D0876094

101

CITIES FOR KIDS

101

CITIES FOR KIDS

Bounty
Books

Publisher: Polly Manguel

Project Editor: Emma Hill

Designer: Ron Callow/Design 23

Production Manager: Neil Randles

First published in Great Britain in 2012 by
Bounty Books, a division of Octopus Publishing Group Limited
Endeavour House,
189 Shaftesbury Avenue,
London WC2H 8JY

www.octopusbooks.co.uk

An Hachette UK Company
www.hachette.co.uk

ISBN: 978-0-753723-08-1

A CIP catalogue record for this book is available from the British
Library

Printed and bound in China

Please note:
We now know that political situations arise very quickly and a city or country that
was quite safe a short time ago can suddenly become a 'no-go' area. Please
check with the relevant authorities before booking tickets and travelling if you
think there could be a problem.

The seasons given in this book relate to the relevant hemisphere. Be sure to
check that you visit at the correct time.

Contents

Introduction

The point where an increasing majority of the human race has migrated from the countryside to dwell industriously in cities has long been reached and passed, dramatically accelerating a process that has been slowly gathering pace since time immemorial. London's population rose from one million to eight million over 130 years during which the British Empire was at its height. Driven by South Korea's Tiger Economy, Seoul took just 25 years to achieve the same expansion, while similar growth is exploding almost everywhere in emerging nations.

There are now well over 300 cities boasting a population of one million or more, plus thousands of smaller ones, and each is of course unique, despite the inescapable fact that globalism has spread the same brands and identical storefronts almost everywhere. But the history of a nation is often woven inextricably into the fabric of its cities, making every city a dynamic fusion of a country's past and present – many booming, some declining, and sadly a few all but forgotten. But each has a tale to tell, offering interested visitors the opportunity to experience its sights and sounds, its people and the lives they live, its heritage and culture, its green enclaves and amusements.

For families with children, deciding to take a holiday in one or more of the great cities is a policy that will prove to be both educational and entertaining. In a world where so much information comes through TV sets and computers, smart phones and the internet, there's actually no substitute for experiencing the real thing at first hand. With so many tempting destinations to choose from, it may be hard to know where to start, so this book describes 101 cities that will reward a family visit. In every case simply being there will be a fascinating eye-opener – in some cases, for children more used to a western way of life, it may be their first experience of the painful reality of poverty evident on the city streets of developing nations. But all the cities in this book not only offer stimulating sightseeing opportunities, but also a wide range of cultural possibilities from magnificent architecture through to great museums.

After getting a real feel for what the place has to offer by way of new experiences, youngsters on holiday also need to let off some steam. So particular attention has been paid to ensuring that every city in the book also offers the kind of attractions that guarantee a fun family holiday which is sure to leave everyone feeling they've had a wonderful time.

EUROPE & THE MIDDLE EAST

Copenhagen

WHEN TO GO:
Explore Copenhagen from late June to early September when the weather is pleasant and evenings are light and long.
TOP FAMILY ATTRACTIONS:
The magnetic Tivoli pleasure gardens where a multi-ride ticket gives access to nearly 30 action adventures; scientific challenges at Experimentarium on the north side that will thrill youngsters of all ages (including dads!) and inspire their interest in nature; the circus revue and breathtaking rides at Bakken amusement park; an interesting display of local marine life (and touching pools) at Øresund aquarium (Øresundsakvariet), located in Elsinore (Helsingør) to the north of Copenhagen.

Dragon Boat Lake, Tivoli Gardens

Wonderful, wonderful... Thanks to the Danny Kaye song, you know what comes next. Copenhagen is a city that should be visited at least once in a lifetime, and you're never too young to do just that. Denmark has the world's oldest monarchy, and the royal family lives in the middle of the city at the Amalienborg Palace. Don't be surprised to see Queen Margrethe out and about, as the royals are famously egalitarian.

A sense of history is everywhere as the family strolls through cobbled squares and narrow streets lined with old buildings, before finding the vast City Hall Square, bounded on one side by the renowned Tivoli Gardens with Strøget (The Straight), Europe's longest pedestrian shopping street, on the other. The square was constructed around 1900 in romantic style. Walk down the broad Strøget and find Gammel Square, with an exquisite bronze fountain erected in 1608; then take a break at an open-air café in Gråbrødre Square at the heart of this trendy shopping area.

There are excellent green parks where families can unwind, and the Tivoli

The balloons in Bakken Amusement park

pleasure gardens offer all sorts of entertaining experiences (especially for those who like roller coasters). Also be sure to show the kids the Little Mermaid, sculpted by Edward Eriksen in 1913 and doomed to sit on her rock in Copenhagen harbour for 300 years before entering the human world (just a couple of centuries to wait, then). She isn't lonely, though, with a million visitors a year.

The New Harbour (Nyhavn, built in the 17th century) is a picturesque waterside area that serves as a starting point for water tours that give a wonderfully different view of this special city. Danish fairy-tale author Hans Christian Andersen lived here for some years, and if children don't already know who he was now's the time to tell them.

YOU SHOULD KNOW:
If pockets have been drained amusing the younger generation, there's free entertainment on offer in the late afternoon and evening, when a variety of street performers come out to play on the Strøget; Bakken (full name Dyrehavsbakken) is the world's oldest amusement park (it has been the scene of popular entertainment since 1583).

Aarhus

Denmark's second-largest city and principal port (often known by the contemporary name of Ärhus) is on the Jutland peninsula. Founded in Viking times, this is the oldest city in Scandinavia. Aarhus takes pride in its heritage, but also in being a thoroughly modern city when it comes to commerce, culture and quality of life. It's a great place to experience the hustle and bustle of Danish city action, with the added bonus that there are plenty of opportunities to find places and activities that will stimulate and excite the younger generation.

There is much to admire about the old. The 15th-century cathedral, dedicated to patron saint of sailors St Clemens, is the tallest, longest church in the country. It has the most frescoes, the biggest organ and Denmark's largest medieval artwork, a triptych. There are fine tombs, early choir stalls and a wonderful altar. It's an experience to remember, and even the kids will be impressed. In the delightful Botanical Gardens may be found Den Gamle By (The Old Town), an atmospheric collection of half-timbered town houses and shops from all over Denmark dating from the 17th to 19th centuries.

The thriving Latin Quarter is beyond the cathedral, a warren of historic streets centred on Pustervig Torv Square with ample opportunities to refuel the family, and another lively place is the colourful Spanish Steps on a waterfront that serves as a magnet for locals (including the city's many students) and tourists alike. There are numerous safe bathing beaches nearby, whilst parks and open spaces abound within the city. The annual summer Aarhus Festuge (Aarhus Party Week) features a different theme each year.

WHEN TO GO:
In July and August, when the city buzzes with open-air life and its green spaces are at their most welcoming.
TOP FAMILY ATTRACTIONS:
Tivoli Friheden amusement park on the south side (and the adjacent wooded World War I memorial park is ideal for a relaxing family picnic); Moesgård Manor House to the south of town, an exceptional museum of prehistory that includes the mummified Grauballe Man from 55 BC (whose throat was cut!); a trip out from town to visit the original Legoland, Denmark's most popular amusement park, located at Billund in Central Denmark (possible by bus, but best to hire a car for the day).
YOU SHOULD KNOW:
For young ones who can be persuaded to take an interest in art and culture, Aros Aarhus Kunstmuseum is an awesome must-visit modern city art gallery, with a classic collection of pictures and installation art to intrigue art-aware kids – but it will be the circular skywalk 'Rainbow Panorama' on the roof of the museum that really grabs them.
For more boisterous fun, head to SegWorld, the world's first indoor off-road Segway park.

The Old Town (Den Gamle By)

The city is dominated by the Lutheran Cathedral.

Helsinki

Until the early 19th century, Helsinki (originally known by the Swedish name of Helsingfors) was an insignificant market town near the mouth of the River Vantaa. Finland was then seized from Sweden by Russia, and Tzar Alexander I made Helsinki its capital. Finland remained under Russian rule until 1918 and the elegant old city dates from the 1830s, when it was built in neoclassical style to resemble St Petersburg, becoming known as 'the white city of the north'.

It is largely on a peninsula linked to widespread suburbs by bridges, causeways and ferries and the sea seems to be around every corner, with trees and rocks forming part of the urban scene. And the old town at the centre seems to offer everything – it is small and intimate with a lively atmosphere, but the pace of life remains relaxed and families are made to feel welcome wherever they go. There's plenty to explore, notably elegant buildings around the central Senate Square, including the enormous Lutheran Cathedral. The South Harbour is a lively spot with its bustling daily market, cafés and the possibility of sightseeing boat trips. From the waterside, walk up the grand Esplanaadikatu boulevard with its excellent shops to discover Mannerheimintie, a main artery for the culturally aware giving access to theatres, galleries, museums and concert halls. Another sight not to be missed is the extraordinary Temppeliaukio Church, built into the living rock and lit by a glazed dome. And boys will love the Suomenlinna fortress complex, built on six islands in the 18th century and now a UNESCO World Heritage Site.

Helsinki also provides interested observers with a fascinating object lesson in modern architecture, featuring some of the 20th century's most iconic modern buildings, such as the Olympic stadium and Finlandia Hall. If that dimension of the city leaves kids (and parents!) unmoved and sight-seeing begins to wear a little thin, there are plenty of family-friendly fun activities to enjoy, plus excellent city parks where youngsters can let off steam.

Sitting on a sea lion can be fun!

15

Oslo

FOLLOWING PAGES: The Viking Ship Museum

Akershus Fortress overlooks Oslo harbour.

Once called Christiania, then Kristiania, Oslo is Norway's capital and largest city. It lies at the head of the Oslofjord, spreading down either side of the water. Oslo's unlucky fourteenth fire destroyed the medieval settlement in 1624 and a new town sprang up around the Akershus Fortress across the water (still a military area today, but open to the public). Oslo is such a force in Norwegian life that it faces criticism for depopulating rural areas by attracting the younger generation – a fact which makes it a lively place which children tend to find rather exciting. Indeed, Oslo regards itself as the party capital of Norway.

Oslo offers much to stimulate culturally inclined families with its world-class museums, galleries, sculpture parks and music venues – not to mention the Nobel Peace Centre, which has an exhibit for every single winner of the prestigious prize. Kids will especially love the tortured paintings of Norway's national genius at the Munch Museum. A stroll along Karl Johans Gate through the heart of the city gives a flavour of Oslo at its best (and that includes shops!). For charming original wooden houses find your way to areas like Kampen, Rodeløkka or Vålerenga. The 17th-century cathedral (Oslo's third) is definitely worth visiting, whilst little princesses with grand designs will love a tour of the sumptuous Royal Palace.

By way of contrast, the centre is surrounded at close quarters by unspoiled wilderness for those who appreciate Nature and want to explore. Oslo is one of the world's largest capitals by area, much of it forest, with 40 islands and 343 lakes within city limits. But of course Norway's party capital is also the country's family entertainment centre, and there are numerous possibilities to stimulate young ones who prefer their thrills served up on a plate.

Gothenburg

Sweden's second-largest city sits astride the Göta Älv River, facing the North Sea, and was planned by Dutch engineers in the 17th century. Gothenburg then became a significant trading harbour and home to the Swedish East India Company. Heavy industry followed in the late 19th and early 20th centuries, though this has declined with consequent economic and social problems. But the place is not nearly as dour as that description might suggest, and is actually regarded as Sweden's friendliest city.

There are reminders of the original town. These include two fortresses – the Skansen Crown in the centre, now a military museum, and the New Älvsborg Fort on an offshore island, a popular tourist attraction. There are splendid 18th century merchants' houses along the canals, including East India House (now Gothenburg City Museum). The 19th century saw the introduction of Landshövdingehusen, unique to Gothenburg. These three-storey buildings have a ground floor built in brick and two upper floors in wood. They evolved to reflect increasing wealth and interest in movements like Art Nouveau, although Gothenburg – in common with much of Scandinavia – eagerly embraced modern architecture in the 20th century.

Gothenburg's main street is known as Avenyn (The Avenue, though officially it's Kungsportsavenyn after a long-demolished city gate). It buzzes with life and is an excellent starting point for shopping, eating or simply relaxing with the kids in one of the many cafés for which the street – and city – are famous. For something different, try the Feskekôrka (literally 'Fish Church' after the building's Gothic exterior), a bustling indoor fish market. The Gothenburg Botanical Garden is one of Europe's finest and there are many large parks and green spaces that don't cost a penny to enjoy. Alternatively, a ferry trip to the picturesque Southern Gothenburg Archipelago can provide a relaxing change of pace.

Gothenburg Harbour

WHEN TO GO:
April to September (many ferry
and other services only
operate in these months and
in winter there are only six
hours of daylight)
TOP FAMILY ATTRACTIONS:
Boat trips on the network of
canals for a different
perspective of this beautiful
city; Junibacken children's
theme park in Djurgården,
recreating the world of Pippi
Longstocking books and Astrid
Lindgren's other tales; Gröna
Lund in the city centre,
Sweden's oldest amusement
park, with spectacular rides
including the fearsome Power
Tower; Vasamuseet, a
maritime museum displaying
the only fully intact 17th
century ship ever salvaged.

Stockholm

Located on Sweden's east coast at the mouth of Lake
Mälaren, Stockholm is a lively city renowned for its
natural beauty, enjoying a spectacular location on 14
islands in the Stockholm Archipelago. Statesman
Birger Jarl erected a fortress on the island of Gamla
Stan in 1252 to defend the passage from the Baltic to
Lake Mälaren. He chose the spot by pushing a log into
the water to see where it would come ashore,
revealing the best location as a harbour for returning
ships. The city's name derives from this: log (stock)
and islet (holm). It became the capital of a
Scandinavian kingdom encompassing modern-day
Sweden, Norway, Denmark, Finland, Iceland and
Greenland. The first King of Sweden, Gustav Vasa,

was crowned in 1523 so Stockholm became (and remains) home to the Swedish royal family.

Stockholm's old town on Gamla Stan retains a medieval plan, with picturesque narrow streets. It is a 'must see'. The city is generally fresh and colourful as most houses are still painted in their original colours: 17th-century buildings are red, 18th-century buildings are yellow, more recent buildings are off-white or grey.

Stockholm boasts several royal palaces that are worth exploring. The largest is the Baroque Drottningholm. Still the residence of the Swedish royal family, it is also a popular tourist attraction with impressive gardens. There are many other wonderful green spaces and the city has over 70 museums. The National Museet has a wide range of fine art, with 16,000 paintings (some by Rembrandt) and 30,000

Skeppsbron waterfront at sunrise, Gamla Stan

YOU SHOULD KNOW:
The city has an excellent public transport network and a Stockholm Card allows unlimited travel and free admission to 80 museums and other sights in Stockholm, plus free sightseeing by boat and other rewarding bonus offers of interest to visitors. But walking is easy (everything is more or less level!) and it's also possible to take self-guided bike tours.

A spectacular exhibit at the Vasamuseet

other works. The Modern Museet features more contemporary works, including those by Picasso and Dalí. The Nordiska Museet is an ethnographical museum dedicated to the culture of Sweden. And when the cultural round is done, the family will discover plenty of interesting places and activities to stimulate and entertain fun-loving kids big and small.

Kaunas

Lithuania's second city is also its industrial powerhouse, located at the confluence of the country's main rivers (the Nemunas and the Neris) close to the vast Kaunas Lagoon. Kaunas is not over-endowed with impressive buildings and picturesque

Laisves aleja (Liberty avenue) in Kaunas with the church of St Michael the Archangel in the distance

25

WHEN TO GO:
Winters are hard, summers warm, so May through September are the best months for a visit.

TOP FAMILY ATTRACTIONS:
A superb panoramic view of the city from the tower of the brand new Resurrection Church, after riding up a funicular railway; the Vytautas, housing the Great War Museum with its incomparable display of weaponry; preserved ruins of Kaunas Castle, including an art gallery in the round tower; Lithuania's only state-run zoo in its oak-grove park; the aquarium at the Mega shopping mall; the Devil's Museum with its thousands of images of Old Nick; a slightly gruesome medical and pharmacy museum.

tourist attractions, and has not recovered from Russian rule as quickly as some. It may not seem like a promising family holiday destination, but actually this somewhat shabby low-rise city is fascinating, with a variety of offbeat curiosities and oddities awaiting discovery.

This is the country's most authentically Lithuanian city. Centuries of foreign occupation have created an ethnically mixed national population, but native Lithuanians make up 93 per cent of the inhabitants of Kaunas compared with just 58 per cent in the capital, Vilnius. For a flavour of the city walk down one of Europe's longest pedestrian streets, Liberty Avenue, continuing along Vilnius Street to explore the oldest part of town.

There are some fascinating historic buildings to see. Kaunas is particularly rich in churches – don't miss the early 15th-century Church of Vytautas the

Great, the monastery and church of Pazaislis, one of the best examples of Italian Baroque architecture in Eastern Europe, St George Church (1487) and the garrison church of St Michael the Archangel. Other notable buildings include the 15th-century red-brick merchant's house of Perkunas and Kaunas Town Hall (nicknamed 'The White Swan') in the old city square. Kaunas has many museums, including art galleries, plus those celebrating matters of local interest. The vast Botanical Garden serves as a showcase for plant life and there are interesting 19th-century Russian fortifications throughout the town, built after local uprisings.

One decided advantage of this bustling city's workaday character is that the family budget will stretch a long way – living costs are very reasonable with hotels, restaurants and attractions offering incredibly low prices. Enjoy!

YOU SHOULD KNOW:
Kaunas welcomed Napoleon's arrival in 1812, hoping it would free Lithuania from Russian rule, and even named a local hill after him.

Surrounded by 15th- and 16th-century merchant houses, Rotuses aikste is the main square in the old city.

Salzburg

WHEN TO GO:
May to June, or September to October (high summer is best avoided by those who like to dodge dense crowds of fellow visitors drawn by the world-famous Salzburg Festival).

TOP FAMILY ATTRACTIONS:
Salzburg Zoo in the south of the city, which in addition to a spectacular menagerie has a petting zoo for children; the thrilling funicular railway ride up to the Hohensalzburg Fortress, which has a great display of early weapons and torture instruments; a well-stocked toy museum (Spielzeugmuseum); the Salzburg Marionette Theatre that performs a large repertoire of operas, ballets and productions for children, using puppets.

YOU SHOULD KNOW:
A Salzburg Card offers unlimited travel and free entry to all the city's attractions. If you're prepared to wait your turn, it's possible to have an amazing game of chess on the giant board painted on the ground near the Cathedral.

FOLLOWING PAGES:
The Alt Stadt and
Hohensalzburg Fortress

Returning to the city
after a great day at the
Hohensalzburg Fortress.

Sometimes, a city is so beautiful that children should simply be encouraged to see it for itself, rather than heading straight for the nearest amusement park. Salzburg, with its world-famous baroque architecture, is just such a place. It has one of the best-preserved city centres in the German-speaking world and is set between the Salzach River and the Mönchsberg in a scenic mountainous area at the northern boundary of the Alps, with mountains to the south and rolling plains to the north. A great way for the family to enjoy Salzburg's visual delights is to take a horse-drawn carriage ride around this impressive city.

Salzburg started out as a Roman town and a Christian kingdom was established by St Rupert in the late 600s. Archbishops of Salzburg soon became hugely powerful and were given the title of Prince of the Holy Roman Empire. The 17th-century Baroque cathedral, the Salzburger Dom, is one of several extraordinary churches in the city. This is where Mozart was baptized. He was born in Salzburg, a fact which is impossible to miss when visiting. The city was not generous towards him during his lifetime but certainly makes the most of him now. Everywhere you go his music is being played, there are two Mozart museums and even chocolate balls called Mozart Kugeln.

A 'must visit' is the Hohensalzburg Fortress, built for those prince-archbishops. It sits on Festungberg Hill and is one of the largest medieval castles in Europe. It is fascinating to appreciate the lavish lifestyle led there, but even better to see truly astonishing views over the Alps and the city. On the other side of the river, the Schloss Mirabell was built in 1606 by Prince-Archbishop Wolf Dietrich for his mistress. It is surrounded by lovely formal gardens and the city has many other parks and green spaces where the family can unwind from architectural overload before heading for the zoo.

Vienna

No Grand Tour of Europe (with or without children) is complete without seeing Austria's vibrant capital, where people still dance the night away to the haunting strains of Strauss waltzes. This fine city sits astride the 'Blue Danube' and was at the heart of the medieval Holy Roman Empire, and later the mighty Hapsburg Austro-Hungarian Empire. Reminders of the city's illustrious past are everywhere – from the Imperial Palace itself to the Hapsburg burial vault and palaces of Belvedere and Schönbrunn, the latter home to Europe's oldest zoo.

Indeed, Vienna has many famous sights, including the world-renowned Spanish Riding School, St Stephen's Cathedral and the Ring Boulevard with its imposing public buildings. With many parks and open

WHEN TO GO:
Vienna is a year-round destination but some attractions (like the Spanish Riding School and Vienna Boys' Choir) take a summer break.

LEFT: The Spanish Riding School

The giant ferris wheel and roller coaster at the Prater amusement park

TOP FAMILY ATTRACTIONS:
Prater amusement park, boasting more than 250 attractions dominated by a giant ferris wheel; Minopolis, Europe's only permanent theme park with an entire city complete in every detail reduced to children's size, looking just like the world of adults in miniature; Danube Tower, offering a panoramic view from the top of this soaring 352-m (1,155-ft) high vantage point with its revolving café-restaurant; the Hofberg, an old treasury that holds the imperial jewels of the Hapsburg dynasty.

Schönbrunn Palace

spaces, Vienna is one of the 'greenest' cities in Europe, offering plenty of opportunity for relaxed picnics or a kickabout to provide a break from sightseeing. One worthwhile family outing is to the Rococo Belvedere Palaces in their park setting, with fine collections of Austrian painting and a stunning alpine garden (best in spring). To enjoy Vienna at its most laid back, every visiting family should pay homage to Danube Island, with its countless restaurants, sports opportunities and sandy river beach.

But Vienna is also renowned for cultural excellence, with splendid theatres, an opera house, museums and a musical tradition that goes far beyond those stirring Strauss Viennese waltzes, with Beethoven and Mozart amongst illustrious former resident composers. On a darker note, Adolf Hitler

also lived here, from 1907 to 1913, trying and failing to enter the Academy of Fine Arts. But he's no more than an unhappy memory, and today's visitors can not only sample the city's traditional and modern architecture and many cultural opportunities, but also enjoy the fine food and vibrant café society for which the city is justly famous.

The famous Christmas
market on Rathausplatz

YOU SHOULD KNOW:
For impressive proof that Vienna moves with the times despite its stunning heritage, take a look at **Hundertwasser House**, an amazing modern apartment building with a grass roof and trees growing out of the windows. Using the city's integrated transport system (underground, high-speed rail, commuter rail, trams and buses) only requires a single ticket but children (up to 14) do not need a ticket on Sundays, holidays and during Austrian school vacations.

Mini-Europe theme park

RIGHT: *The Belgian
Centre for Comic
Strip Art*

Brussels

Brussels punches above its weight – not only is this cosmopolitan city Belgium's capital, but also the political headquarters of both the North Atlantic Treaty Organisation (NATO) and the European Union (EU). But despite all those bureaucrats it remains a lively destination with much to offer visiting families.

Brussels flourished from the 15th century as Princely Capital of the Low Countries, an integral and important part of the mighty Holy Roman Empire, and has retained a strong sense of historical tradition. Belgium gained independence in 1830 and the city was largely redeveloped at the end of the 19th century. Few of the original buildings survived, though a shining exception at the city's heart is a magnificent cobbled market square, the Grand Place, which features some wonderful old guild houses and the extraordinary Gothic city hall, all spectacularly lit at night.

Other worthwhile historic buildings include two Royal Palaces (of Laeken and Brussels), the Cathedral of Saint Michael and Saint Gudula, the Basilica of the Sacred Heart and the classically fronted Stock Exchange. And of course no tourist can ever leave Brussels without seeing the world's most famous bronze statue – that slightly naughty and permanently tinkling Manneken Pis, always a big hit with youngsters. Another well-known icon is the recently renovated Atomium, representing an iron crystal, dating from the World Expo of 1958.

With over a hundred museums, the strength of Brussels is cultural rather than architectural, although visitors interested in neither will find plenty to entertain them. Shoppers can visit the elegant Galeries Saint Hubert, a superb early Victorian shopping arcade, anyone who likes chocolate will soon be putting on weight and there are plenty of attractions to amuse and entertain children.

WHEN TO GO:
With few outdoor attractions, Brussels is an all-year-round destination, though winter weather can be raw.

TOP FAMILY ATTRACTIONS:
The Belgian Centre for Comic Strip Art, covering a full range of comic art, especially locals like Tintin and Snowy or the Smurfs; Mini-Europe theme park next to the Atomium, featuring miniature replicas of many famous European buildings; free summer parties in the central Brussels Park, close to the Belgian parliament; Scientastic, where kids aged six and over will think science is fun after a couple of interactive hours (a rainy-day winner).

YOU SHOULD KNOW:
Love them or hate them, most families will not know or care whether or not those sprouts really came originally from Brussels, but it is possible to learn something new every day. They did.

Carcassonne

WHEN TO GO:
Any time, but some outdoor attractions are closed in winter (November to February); July and August for those wanting to enjoy the Cité Festival, with performances held in the extraordinary open-air theatre in the old city.
TOP FAMILY ATTRACTIONS:
A guided tour of the old city and castle (including rampart ride); Raymond Chésa Leisure Park situated in extensive natural surroundings close to the imposing walls of the old city, offering great walks and activities such as pedalos, mini golf, beach volleyball courts and a forest adventure park; a boat trip on the picturesque Canal du Midi; Parc Australien for a French take on 'Down Under', featuring kangaroos and emus, gold prospectors and aborigines, boomerangs and didgeridoos; Cité des Oiseaux (Bird City) for stunning aerial displays by trained birds of prey and others (oh, and there are wolves too).
YOU SHOULD KNOW:
It's possible to make use of free electrically powered vehicles called 'Toucs' (with drivers) which tour the lower town.

Visiting some cities is fun for families, a visit to others is a fascinating education. Carcassonne in the Languedoc is definitely in the latter category – at least one Carcassonne is (that would be the amazing ancient walled settlement on a rocky outcrop). But there's another Carcassonne (the more recent but still historic lower city) which nowadays offers more modern satisfactions. But this isn't a tale of two cities – for actually the two count as one, despite the fact that they are clearly separate entities.

The fortified city – Cité de Carcassonne – is a UNESCO World Heritage Site and has a double ring of massive ramparts with 53 towers. Medieval walls are built on Roman foundations, emphasizing the importance of Carcassonne in historical times, standing as it does in a gap between the Massif Central and the Pyrenees where two great routes cross (Atlantic to Mediterranean, Massif Central to Spain). It became an important trading centre that changed hands frequently by marriage or force of arms. The old city was scheduled for demolition in the 19th century, but saved after a local campaign and restored over many years, not altogether authentically. Even so, the effect is stunning. Only a few hundred people live there now, many of them traditional craftspeople. Just stroll around enjoying the walls, towers, 12th-century castle, Cathedral (Basilica-Saint-Nazarius, begun in the 11th century) and ancient streets.

The lower city (Ville Basse) across the River Aude was founded by King Louis IX in 1247, after Carcassonne submitted to French rule. This medieval city grew rich on the manufacture of shoes and textiles, declined in the 17th century and nowadays thrives on tourism – three million visitors arrive to see the old city each year, supplemented by those cruising the wonderful Canal du Midi (also a UNESCO World Heritage Site). The medieval heart of modern Carcassonne (Bastide Saint-Louis) is itself a delightful enclave centred on Place Carnot with its Fountain of Neptune (1770) and traditional market.

FOLLOWING PAGES: The spectacular old city of Carcassonne

Walking the ramparts.

Nantes

The most important city in historic Brittany (from which it has been separated since 1941) has an enviable reputation as one of the most pleasant places to live in France. It is also a wonderful destination for a family visit, offering attractions old and new. Nantes is located where the Loire, Erdre and Sèvre Rivers merge, close to the Atlantic, and was at the centre of the French colonial trade – historic Quai de la Fosse

still serving as a reminder of those prosperous days.

France's sixth-largest city is a clean, well-run place with beautiful cobbled streets, numerous fine buildings, interesting monuments, great museums, refreshing parks and a lively arts scene...all energized by the large student population. Intense postwar redevelopment (some rather ordinary) has somewhat diluted the character of the old city. But there is still plenty to admire in an architectural context, and Nantes has many national monuments, including one that will have all self-respecting children literally salivating.

The stunning Château des Ducs de Bretagne is everything a feudal French castle should be. The Gothic Cathedral of Saints Peter and Paul is close by (don't miss the black-and-white marble tomb within). Bouffay is the ancient medieval quarter near the Cathedral. The area around the Place du Commerce shows French 19th-century architecture at its best, whilst the semicircular Place Graslin contains a neoclassical opera house. A smart shopping area in and around Rue Crébillon has the unique Passage Pommeraya as its star item – an extraordinary three-level 19th-century arcade. A symbol of 21st-century urban regeneration is the Île de Nantes, a former shipyard and dockland on a Loire river island, now being redeveloped as the new civic centre with warehouses converted into visitor attractions. And that tempt-the-kids national monument? Traditional chocolatier Gautier Debotté in Rue de la Foss, with its amazing interior and beguiling wares. Nantes is also a great base from which to visit nearby attractions such as Futuroscop and Puy du Fou.

WHEN TO GO:
The end of March (or thereabouts) for the floats, dancers and street artists of the Nantes Carnival. Summers are mild and winters cool.

TOP FAMILY ATTRACTIONS:
The cliffside Jules Verne Museum, paying homage to the vivid imagination of this 19th-century writer, a son of Nantes; contemporary arts centre Le Lieu Unique, with great views from the tower;

Les Machines De L'île, a creative metropole of dream and of fantasy headlined by a huge mechanical elephant and marine-world carousel; a trip out of town to one of France's top visitor attractions, Puy du Fou on the coast, to experience a whirlwind of exciting medieval recreations; Espace Quilly between Nantes and La Baule for older kids (jet skiing, quad biking and prestige cars for dads to try); Futuroscope, near Poitiers to the south but easily reached from Nantes, a sensational future-themed amusement park.

YOU SHOULD KNOW:
There's a local speciality that can come to the rescue of parents when children (inevitably) become tired of culture and start complaining that they're hungry. Galettes are a less sweet version of the crepe and can be eaten at any time of the day, filled with meat, eggs, cheese, or a variety of other tasty things.

The mechanical elephant at the Machines de L'île

43

Paris ✓

Everyone should experience this global city sitting astride the River Seine – and you're never too young to start. As might be expected of the world's most popular tourist destination, Paris tests the superlatives with amazing architecture, incredible museums, world-class galleries, fabulous parks, great theatres, elegant boulevards, classy shops, gourmet restaurants, lively cafés...and the iconic Eiffel Tower. This is the city's symbol, and those willing to climb 700-odd stairs (and travel on by lift) see a stunning city panorama that has been enjoyed by over 200 million people since the tower opened in 1887. It was the world's tallest structure until New York's Chrysler building was topped out in 1930.

Paris has a list of landmarks that goes on and on – Cathédrale-Notre-Dame (of Hunchback fame), Arc de Triomphe, Champs-Elysées, Sacré Coeur, Les Invalides, Panthéon, Opéra Garnier, Grande Arche...

Children looking up at the very tall Eiffel Tower.

and many more. To those may be added museums like the Louvre, Musée National d'Art Moderne, Musée d'Orsay...the list goes on. Then there are famous quarters like the Rive Gauche, Faubourg Saint-Honoré, L'Opéra, Montmartre, Les Halles, Quartier Latin, Montparnasse...all with a unique appeal of their own. Not to mention fabulous parks and green spaces – the Tuileries, the Luxembourg Gardens on the Left Bank, the Bois de Boulogne to name but a few.

Yes, it's overwhelming – but actually that doesn't matter. There's so much to see, do and enjoy that it would be impossible to cram everything into a lifetime, let alone one visit. So the answer is simple – go with the flow in the knowledge that wherever it takes you, you will enjoy a rewarding experience. Then promise the children a return visit next year. For along with all that history and culture Paris boasts some fabulous attractions that will stimulate and excite the younger generation.

Sleeping Beauty's castle at Disneyland Paris

WHEN TO GO:
In the springtime, of course, but canny crowd-haters know the city gets emptier for a month from 15 July for annual holidays.

TOP FAMILY ATTRACTIONS:
The opportunity to smile back at the world's most famous picture – Leonardo Da Vinci's enigmatic Mona Lisa (*La Gioconda*) in the Louvre; the slightly creepy Catacombs – mass tombs in underground limestone passages that were the city's late-18th-century solution to overcrowded cemeteries; Jardin d'Acclimatation in the northern part of the Bois de Boulogne, a children's amusement park with menagerie, Exploradôme museum and other attractions; Disneyland Paris speaks for itself, but is actually some 32km (20mi) from the centre of town; La Mer de Sable (April to September), a lively theme park 65km (40 miles) from the centre of Paris that's well worth the journey; Parc Asterix (April to November), 35 km (22 mi) north of town, known for its roller coasters plus historic rides with Roman and Ancient Greek themes.

YOU SHOULD KNOW:
To fully appreciate the city's unique atmosphere the best (and cheapest!) way to get around Paris is on foot. But the famous Metro is an excellent way of covering the wider city or transporting the family to fringe locations, with an inexpensive ticket allowing a one-way trip of any length.

Enjoying the fountains outside the Louvre.

Leipzig

Like all major German cities, Leipzig took a fearful pounding from Allied bombers in World War II, before becoming incorporated into the GDR (East Germany). The Leipzig Trade Fair was an important annual event during the Communist years, providing a contact point between east and west, but was actually the continuation of a much older tradition – this Saxon city was granted two annual market fairs back in the 12th century, contributing mightily to Leipzig's importance and success as a trading centre over the centuries.

It might be supposed that war damage and subsequent neglect left the city with a huge and burdensome legacy at the time of German reunification in 1990, but to everyone's surprise Leipzig hit the ground running and quickly established itself as a place that is well worth exploring – regaining its traditional status as a stylish regional centre of trade, education and culture, with excellent shops and a vibrant social scene. This has ensured that the city receives plenty of visitors young and older, all of whom find plenty of worthwhile things to see and do.

Although many buildings date from both before and after the fall of Communism (the former rather dull, the latter often ultra-modern), with more on the way, the compact city centre seems remarkably unspoiled. There are fine churches, extraordinary covered market passages galore (Mädler-Passage is especially good), one of Germany's oldest universities and the medieval Renaissance Market Square, overlooked by a splendid 16th-century Old Town Hall (now a fascinating museum). Here also you will find the Gothic Church of St Thomas (Thomaskirche) where the great composer Johann Sebastian Bach served as cantor and was buried. There's even an adjacent Bach Museum for serious musicologists, although visitors with children may well prefer more light-hearted diversions, including hanging loose in one of the city's many riverside parks.

WHEN TO GO:
May to September are the months to make the most of the city and its many open-air possibilities.

TOP FAMILY ATTRACTIONS:
Panorama Tower, Augustusplatz, Leipzig's highest building, offering a great view of town from an observation platform at the top; Leipzig Zoo, founded in the 19th century and now offering state-of-the-art enclosures and unusual sights like elephants bathing – from an underwater viewpoint; the slightly chilling Museum in der Runden Ecke, formerly HQ of the dreaded Stasi secret police, now a museum exploring bad old GDR days; a museum dedicated to Leipzig's comprehensive and long-established electric tramway system (pre-planning required – open only one day a month from May to September but well worth the effort, especially if there are boys in the family); Belantis amusement park for all the family, 10 km (6 mi) from the city centre, featuring roller coasters, boat and water rides and other amusements (April to October).

YOU SHOULD KNOW:
Leipzig's amazing Christmas market (late November and on into December) is effectively a major winter-themed carnival with assorted attractions, including a ferris wheel. Auerbach's Cellar is Leipzig's oldest restaurant – Goethe drank there as a student and included the place in his play *Faust*, where it was visited by Mephistopheles and Faust.

Belantis amusement park is a short distance from the city.

Munich

WHEN TO GO:
Alpine weather is unpredictable, but the summer months (May to September) are pretty reliable. Thereafter, Oktoberfest (yes, in October!) is worth seeing – lasting for two weeks, it's known as the 'largest people's fair in the world'. Later still a Christmas Market is held in Marienplatz from the beginning of advent until Christmas Eve.

Children looking at a hot air balloon exhibit at the Deutsches Museum.

Germany's third-largest city lies on the River Isar north of the Bavarian Alps. It began with a monastery and river crossing in the 12th century, with the Dukes of Bavaria ruling continuously until 1918. Munich's history after World War 1 was turbulent, starting with a Communist uprising and ending in domination by Hitler's Nazi party, which regarded the city as its heartland. Several so-called 'Führer buildings' were erected around Königsplatz, where rallies were held (only two remain today).

Following World War II, traditional rebuilding left this monumental city looking much as it had done before, with a compact but stunning inner city that's

A giraffe in Hellabrunn Zoo attracts a lot of attention.

well worth exploring. Spacious Marienplatz lies at the centre, containing old and new town halls. Three medieval city gates survive, one – Karlstor – being the oldest structure in Stachus, a square that contains the Palace of Justice. There are splendid churches to be found, like the Romanesque St Peter's, Munich's oldest, or the 15th-century Cathedral of Our Lady (Frauenkirche). On the edge of the old town is the magnificent Royal Residence (Residenz), now a fabulous museum.

51

TOP FAMILY ATTRACTIONS:
BMW Museum featuring engines and turbines, aircraft, motorcycles and vehicles galore; Deutsches Museum, the world's largest museum of technology and science with approximately 28,000 exhibits; Hellabrun Zoo, one of the largest in Europe (and an aquarium – don't miss the piranha feeding); regular performances at the enchanting Münchner Marionettentheater (puppet theatre); Bavaria Film, offering fascinating studio tours.

YOU SHOULD KNOW:
The view from the top of the Cathedral's south tower can't be spoiled – no taller building can be erected in the city.

The BMW Museum

Four grand 19th-century avenues run out from the centre. The neoclassical Brienner Strasse opens into the imposing Königsplatz, now a gallery and museum quarter. The Italianate Ludwigstrasse has many fine public buildings. Neo-Gothic Maximilianstrasse encompasses some of Munich's most expensive shops. Lastly, Prinzregentenstrasse with its many museums sweeps across the river. Away from the centre, several palaces are to be found.

In fact, Munich has attractions architectural and otherwise too numerous to list, including many parks, wonderful buildings, interesting museums and lively street life. If the family only visits one German city, make it this one...and stay for a week. Munich may be the country's most expensive city, but the experience is worth every penny.

Amsterdam

Amsterdam started out in the 13th century as a small fishing village. According to legend, it was founded by two fishermen who landed on the shores of the Amstel river in a small boat with their dog. The damming of the river gave the village its name. Today it is the capital of the Netherlands, known for liberal attitudes, vibrant culture and rich history. The city has endless attractive canals, some truly great art collections, stunning architecture and fascinating museums, so an enquiring family could easily spend a week or more exploring (and enjoying) this great city.

Few very early buildings survive but those that do are special – including the medieval Oude Kerk (Old Church, with little houses on its sides), the Neuwe Kerk (New Church) and the Houten Huis (Wooden House). The centre was largely built during the Golden Age in the 17th century, when Amsterdam was one of the world's wealthiest cities, with trade links to the Baltic, North America, Africa, Indonesia and Brazil. This period saw the building of the classical Royal Palace on Damplein, the Westerkerk, Zuiderkerk and many notable canal houses, including De Dolfijn (Dolphin) and De Gecroonde Raep (Crowned Turnip).

For the culturally inclined, Amsterdam has outstanding museums, including the Rijksmuseum, the Stedelijk Museum and the Rembrandt House Museum. The

WHEN TO GO:
Between May and September
TOP FAMILY ATTRACTIONS:
Anne Frank House on the Prinsengracht – the former hiding place where Anne wrote her famous diary, which is among the original objects on display; a boat tour of the canals, a great way to see the city's best sights; Artis, short for Natura Artis Magistra (Latin for 'Nature is the teacher of art') in the centre of Amsterdam, the oldest zoo in the Netherlands; the awesome-looking waterside NEMO science centre with lots of interactive action to stimulate the kids; a trip out of town to the Archeon living museum (between Amsterdam and Den Haag) for informative and entertaining animation of Dutch history and former ways of life (open from April to October and at Christmas).

Children enjoying an interactive exhibit at the NEMO Science Centre.

Van Gogh Museum houses the largest collection of the artist's work in the world. Amsterdam is also famous for canals. The three main canals extend from the IJ Lake, and each marks the position of moated city walls in different historic periods. The innermost is the Herengracht (Lord's Canal). Beyond it lie the

Keizersgracht (Emperor's Canal) and the Prinsengracht (Prince's Canal). The banks are best explored on foot, or by bicycle. Smaller canals intersect the main ones, dividing the city into numerous islands, and nearly 1,300 bridges criss-cross the waterways of this beautiful city known as 'Venice of the North'.

Prinsengracht (Prince's Canal)

Fasnacht – Basel's carnival is a great experience.

Basel

Switzerland's third-largest city lies on the River Rhine, close to both Germany and France, and is a major industrial centre. It is a railway hub, with three main stations – one each for the Swiss, German and French networks. Five bridges connect the two halves of the city (known as Greater and Lesser Basel), but it's well worth crossing on one of the old-fashioned cable ferries.

A stroll round the city reveals many stunning examples of modern architecture, including the

Messeturm, Switzerland's tallest building. But there is historic character aplenty. The medieval town centre in Greater Basel is a delight, and contains splendid buildings like the red sandstone Minster Church on impressive Minster Square (minster is an alternative term for cathedral). This early gothic building was reconstructed after the great earthquake of 1356. The grand Renaissance town hall on the market square (Marktplatz, where there's still a daily market) is also noteworthy. A maze of narrow traffic-free cobbled streets demands to be explored, though parents may struggle to keep up with their offspring – the gradients are steep!

Basel prides itself as a city of culture, with some 40 museums (most with free entry towards the end of the day), a dozen theatres and regular concerts in churches and the open air. But the city is really famous for the Basel Carnival (Fasnacht), the country's largest and one of the world's best. It starts at precisely four o'clock in the morning on the Monday after Ash Wednesday, the first day of Lent, and lasts 72 hours to the minute (they're Swiss, after all). Up to 20,000 revellers wear masks and colourful costumes and there are numerous parades, marching bands, concerts and lantern displays, and all the while a huge amount of confetti rains down. A great experience for families who plan their visit with Fasnacht in mind!

WHEN TO GO:
Basel is best enjoyed on foot, ideally during the temperate months of May to September.
TOP FAMILY ATTRACTIONS:
Amazing animated mechanical sculptures by Jean Tinguely and like-minded kinetic artists (kids love them) at the museum that bears his name; Zolli, the popular name for Basel Zoological Garden, one of the world's best zoos (don't miss the monkeys solving problems to earn their food); the boys had it all their way at Munich's BMW Museum, so now the girls get their turn at the Doll's house Museum at Barfüsserplatz in the city centre, with over 6,000 exhibits including teddy bears, dolls, play shops and wonderful doll's houses; a shortish trip out of town and across into Germany to enjoy the amazing Europa amusement park, home to some sensational rides including the awesome Blue Fire (limited winter opening, access from the A5 road to Karlsruhe).
YOU SHOULD KNOW:
Most Swiss homes harbour an assault rifle, in case the citizen army is needed to repel surprise invaders (don't be unduly alarmed, because happily armies of incoming tourists are not classed as a threat to national security).

57

Bristol

Like other British cities, Bristol experienced difficult times when its traditional role declined. The city's famous Floating Harbour fell out of use and port activity moved to nearby Avonmouth and Royal Portbury Dock. However, recent regeneration has transformed Bristol's waterfront into a lively location that contributes to this great city's growing reputation as a visitor-friendly destination...for all the family.

Bristol thrived as a port for Irish trade, but the 18th-century slave trade really made the city's fortune. Later, the city became indelibly associated with the great engineer Isambard Kingdom Brunel, who designed iconic Clifton Suspension Bridge, built pioneering iron steamships and created the Great Western Railway between Bristol and London.

Wealthy residential areas like Clifton are rich in the finest Georgian architecture, but the city centre was destroyed by bombing in World War II and is now a park containing ruined churches and fragmentary remains of Bristol Castle. Fortunately, enough of Old Bristol survived to retain a strong sense of the city's historic character. The Georgian House in Robert Adam's urban masterpiece, Charlotte Square, is believed to be the place where poets Wordsworth and Coleridge first met. College Green is a fine public open space surrounded by interesting buildings, including Bristol's fine 12th-century Cathedral. The New Room is actually the oldest Methodist chapel in the world, built by the movement's founder John Wesley in 1739. Bristol City Museum and Art Gallery has an outstanding general collection in a fine building donated by the prominent local Wills tobacco family.

With a large student population and strong commercial life, Bristol is a bustling city with lively street life that is reinventing itself for the 21st century, whilst paying more attention to preserving a heritage that was until recently under threat. Well worth a family visit!

WHEN TO GO:
Summer is a good time to appreciate Bristol's waterside attractions.
TOP FAMILY ATTRACTIONS:
Bristol Zoological Gardens, the world's oldest provincial zoo (founded in 1836), now specializing in rare and endangered species and innovative displays; the harbourside Bristol Aquarium (everything from sharks to seahorses, plus underwater glass tunnels); M-Shed for a museum of Bristol life, plus Harbour Railway – ride on a Bristol-built locomotive and be transported back to the days of steam (March to October); Brunel's restored iron passenger ship SS *Great Britain*, now an award-winning attraction in the dock where she was originally built in 1843; the city's ice-skating rink; Avon Valley Adventure Park at nearby Keynsham for family adventure, fun and animals (April to October).
YOU SHOULD KNOW:
Renowned (and somewhat anonymous) graffiti artist Banksy is a Bristolian, and quite a number of his wonderfully imaginative (and subversive) early wall paintings may be seen at various locations around the city, including works such as *Graffiti Sniper* and *Cat & Dog*.

Two girls looking at tropical fish at Bristol Aquarium.

Chester

WHEN TO GO:
Summer, to enjoy the walk around those famous city walls in the best possible weather, although they will be crowded in high season (mid-July to the end of August).

TOP FAMILY ATTRACTIONS:
Chester Zoo, voted one of the world's best with extensive grounds and 7,000 animals; the Grosvenor Museum for fascinating displays that bring Roman Chester alive, and the chance to explore domestic life from the 17th century to the 1920s; riding the miniature railway in Grosvenor Park (April to October); Cheshire Military Museum at the castle; Gulliver's World Resort at nearby Warrington, with 37 rides and 60 attractions designed to thrill and entertain children up to the age of 13 (limited winter opening); a trip out of town to Jodrell Bank Discovery Centre near Macclesfield for enquiring young scientific minds who will enjoy the Planet and Space pavilions.

YOU SHOULD KNOW:
Make the kids shiver by telling them that in 1656 three witches (Ellen Beech, Anne Osboston and Ann Thornton) were hanged on Gallows Hill and buried in St Mary's-on-the-Hill churchyard.

Cheshire's county town is on the River Dee, close to Wales – though traditionally there is no love lost between Chester's inhabitants (Cestrians) and the Welsh. The city is one of the best-preserved walled cities in England. The walls are almost complete – constructed from as early as 120 AD, they enclose the inner city with only two short breaks. There couldn't be a better way to show youngsters how towns were defended in ancient times, and there's much more living history besides.

Chester was a significant Roman centre, and evidence of their presence may still be seen – notably the amphitheatre and reconstructed Roman Garden complete with hypocaust (heating system). The city remained important because of its strategic location as a jumping-off point for Ireland. It was a river port and trading centre until overtaken by Liverpool, after which it became a fashionable Georgian retreat from industrial northwest England.

The word 'Grosvenor' appears frequently in Chester, being the family name of the Dukes of Westminster who own much of the property here. Chester's characteristic medieval half-timbered appearance was enhanced by the Victorian remodelling instituted by the first duke, though many 17th-century originals remain. Distinctive features of estate-owned buildings are twisted chimneys and grey-brick diamonds within red brickwork, still much in evidence. There is a medieval cathedral and Norman castle, too.

In common with many British cities, there was rapid development after World War II, often at the expense of historic buildings. This generated considerable change in central Chester, but ended with a switch of emphasis to conservation in the late 1960s. Although now surrounded by extensive suburbs, the bustling centre is enticing, retaining a pleasing variety of architecture that includes the unique Rows – a series of half-timbered buildings joined with long galleries, looking for all the world like Tudor shopping malls, with splendid examples to be seen in Watergate, Eastgate and Bridge Street.

FOLLOWING PAGES:
A scenic view of
Eastgate Street from
the city walls

A pair of strolling
jaguars at Chester Zoo

61

Looking out at St Paul's Cathedral from the Tate Modern.

WHEN TO GO:
London is an all-year destination, but does not look at its best during the sometimes-dreary winter months (November-March).

TOP FAMILY ATTRACTIONS:
First among equals – the Tower of London; beautiful parks, notably Regent's Park with its wonderful zoo and Hyde Park with the Princess Diana Memorial; the Imperial War Museum – also HMS *Belfast*, a World War II cruiser moored near Tower Bridge; an excursion out to Windsor Castle, home to Queen Mary's fabulous doll's house; the spooky London Dungeon; a river trip down the Thames from Westminster to Greenwich; SEA LIFE London aquarium with 14 themed zones; a sightseeing open-topped bus tour; Chessington World of Adventures, a major theme park with numerous rides and attractions, plus a zoo and aquarium (a short train ride out of town, limited winter opening).

London

The United Kingdom's capital is one of the world's greatest cities – a place redolent with history. London is a renowned global centre of business, finance and culture, with huge influence over international affairs. That need not unduly concern families who plan to visit the vibrant metropolis, for London is also a major tourist destination with attractions too numerous to list, including four UNESCO World Heritage Sites (the Tower of London, Maritime Greenwich, the Royal Botanic Gardens at Kew and Westminster Abbey/Palace with St Margaret's Church).

In addition, London has numerous iconic sights

such as Buckingham Palace, Tower Bridge, Big Ben, the Houses of Parliament, the high-flying London Eye (ride it!), Nelson's Column in Trafalgar Square, St Paul's Cathedral, Marble Arch and Piccadilly Circus. There are a host of significant civic buildings, wonderful churches and magnificent Georgian and Victorian architecture.

The city was destroyed by the Great Fire of 1666, famously beginning in Pudding Lane, so few earlier buildings remain. Extensive bomb damage was sustained in World War II, and piecemeal postwar development has resulted in mixed architectural styles that give London its special character. The original City of London, the financial district, is home to striking modern buildings, as is the Isle of Dogs beyond – formerly derelict dockland that now rivals the old City. Further east, massive regeneration was triggered by the award of the 2012 Olympic Games.

World-class cultural facilities include the British Museum, Natural History Museum, Science Museum, Victoria and Albert Museum, National Gallery, National Portrait Gallery, Tate Britain and Tate Modern. London is also the country's entertainment capital, with numerous theatres and concert halls. It's a retail therapist's paradise, too, as the West End (including Oxford Street and Regent Street) vies with classy Knightsbridge to offer the ultimate shopping experience. Visiting families need answer only one question – 'how much time can you spare/afford?'.

The Houses of Parliament from a pod on the London Eye

FOLLOWING PAGES: A view of the National Maritime Museum in Greenwich from Observatory Hill

Admiring a statue at the Victoria and Albert Museum.

York

One of Britain's most important Roman settlements, York was subsequently occupied by Anglo-Saxons and Vikings. It remained an important religious and commercial centre throughout the Middle Ages, declining only when the Industrial Revolution passed it by. York thus kept much of its medieval heritage, unlike many northern towns that were redeveloped in the 19th century to serve the burgeoning needs of industry. This is therefore one of the most stunning medieval cities in England, and a visit is guaranteed to satisfy families with children young or older.

York Minster is the largest Gothic cathedral in northern Europe. There has been a church on the site since the 7th century, although the cathedral was largely rebuilt from the 13th century. It was consecrated in 1472, serving as a reminder that the great cathedrals we so admire often took several lifetimes to complete. Since then, the Minster has suffered several disastrous fires and renovation continues. Its Great East Window contains the largest expanse of medieval stained glass in the world.

The compact old city, enclosed by well-preserved gated walls that may be walked for excellent city views, is a delight to explore. A medieval centre has charming streets like the famous Shambles and numerous pedestrian alleys called snickelways. These often have eccentric names like Lady Peckett's Yard or Mad Alice Lane. Merchant Adventurers' Hall is Europe's finest medieval guildhall, containing a hospital and chapel in the undercroft with a magnificent timbered Great Hall above. Barley Hall is a restored medieval gem in Coffee Yard, a snickelway off Stonegate. York's Norman castle has been dismantled, but Clifford's Tower (a quatrefoil keep) remains and the site contains later buildings – courts, a former prison and an interesting museum. York has many old churches, mostly medieval, and for those into organized activities, one of York's many regular festivals is usually in progress.

York Minster Cathedral and the city wall

Cardiff

Until development of the South Wales coal industry in the 19th century, Cardiff was a small coastal town with modest trading and fishing interests. That soon changed, with the town becoming a major port, a city in 1905 and capital of Wales in 1955. Cardiff is the political, cultural, sporting and economic centre of a proud nation that is spreading its wings, and this great city has recently experienced a significant,

The striking Millennium Centre serves predominantly as a theatre and opera house.

ongoing and long overdue regeneration programme.

As every visitor who samples Cardiff's vibrant atmosphere will testify, that programme is succeeding. Sparkling modern architecture is springing up everywhere – just look at the Welsh Assembly, Wales Millennium Centre, Millennium Stadium or the extraordinary 'Tube', actually Cardiff Bay Visitor Centre, where it's possible to see a scale model of the evolving city. These and other developments reinforce Cardiff's credentials as an exciting modern city that's

WHEN TO GO:
May to September, as there are many outdoor attractions to enjoy in Cardiff. There's an excellent free festival in July and August.

TOP FAMILY ATTRACTIONS:
Cardiff International White Water for thrilling action for all ages, including white-water rafting, kayaking and hydro speeding; Techniquest, the hands-on science centre at Cardiff Bay waterfront that will fascinate and engage children and parents both; Barry Island Pleasure Park south of Cardiff for old-fashioned seaside fun; St Fagans National History Museum – a large park outside town containing historic buildings brought from all over Wales; for sports fans young and old – a tour of the Millennium Stadium (not on match days!), to include a walk down the players' tunnel and short rest on the Queen's seat in the Royal Box; Castell Coch to the north of the city, a wonderful Victorian Gothic Revival castle built on genuine 13th-century foundations.

YOU SHOULD KNOW:
Famous children's author Roald Dahl was christened at Cardiff's charming Norwegian Church, now a café and art gallery. The Cardiff OYbike scheme has 17 convenient, automated, 24/7 bicycle rental locations – providing an eco-friendly way to tour the city.

A young boy touching a lightning globe at Techniquest Science Museum.

RIGHT: A picnic outside Castell Coch

going places fast, and the energy is palpable.

There's still plenty of heritage for those who prefer more traditional attractions. Llandaff Cathedral has been a focal point since it was begun in the 12th century, and now sits at the heart of a peaceful conservation area close to the River Taff. Cardiff's splendid Catholic Cathedral dates from 1887. Must-see Cardiff Castle incorporates Roman remains, a Norman keep and lavish interiors created during 19th-century refurbishment for the ultra-rich Marquis of Bute. He also donated the park named after him, adjacent to the castle, which is a large green area at the heart of the city.

Those of athletic bent may be interested in hiring bikes and cycling a section of the Taff Trail, a scenic off-road cycleway connecting Cardiff to Brecon, but the city presents plenty of less strenuous (and tempting!) opportunities for entertainment. Whether sport, history or culture is your thing, there are plenty of attractions in Cardiff and the surrounding areas for all the family.

Glasgow

In the eternal rivalry between Scotland's two greatest cities, Glasgow in the wild west claims commercial superiority over Edinburgh in the elegant east. The latter would claim to be the destination of choice for visiting families with cultural improvement in mind, but Glasgow combines its own rich cultural heritage with opportunities for rip-roaring fun.

Glasgow prospered from the 18th century, becoming a world leader in engineering and shipbuilding during the Industrial Revolution and earning the title 'Second City of the British Empire'. Today, this sprawling city on the River Clyde has half the population it once boasted, thanks to slum clearances and the creation of overspill towns. The decline of traditional heavy industries led to serious deprivation and urban decay, but a vigorous regeneration programme, beginning with Glasgow's status as a European Capital of Culture in 1990, has turned the tide and made this lively city a very rewarding destination.

Historic Glasgow was focused on St Mungo's Cathedral, one of Scotland's few medieval churches, and the old High Street down past Glasgow Cross intersection to the river. This area fell into decay as the centre moved westwards. It is now bounded by the High Street, river and intrusive M8 motorway, but is being reinvented as a bohemian quarter. George Square is at the heart of the modern city, surrounded by Scotland's most important retail area – Argyle, Buchanan and Sauchiehall Streets, sometimes known as 'The Golden Z'.

Many of Glasgow's cultural treasures may be found in the centre of this monumental Victorian city, though the amazing Burrell Collection

WHEN TO GO:
During the warmer months – May to September – but be prepared for (unrelenting) rain at any time.
TOP FAMILY ATTRACTIONS:
The Riverside Museum and nearby Tall Ship in Glasgow Harbour; Glasgow Science Centre beside the Clyde providing an educational yet exciting interactive experience (also has an IMAX cinema and lofty viewing tower); The Museum of Transport in the Kelvin Hall, using its superb collections of vehicles and models to tell the story of transport by land and sea, with a unique Glasgow spin; a longish but very worthwhile trip out of town to Blair Drummond Safari & Adventure Park (train to Stirling then bus).
YOU SHOULD KNOW:
Daniel Defoe of *Robinson Crusoe* fame called Glasgow 'the cleanest and beautifullest and best built city in Britain, London excepted'.

There is so much to see at Kelvingrove Art Gallery and Museum.

75

Glasgow Science Centre on the banks of the River Clyde houses the IMAX Cinema and Glasgow Tower.

containing the astonishing acquisitions of a Victorian shipping magnate is in Pollok Country Park. Other notable venues include Kelvingrove Art Gallery and Museum on Argyle Street, opened in 1901 to house one of Europe's finest civic art collections, and GoMA (Gallery of Modern Art) – ironically housed in a fine 18th-century building.

Dublin ✓

In Dublin's fair city, the girls are still pretty...and that's true of Dublin itself, despite ill-considered redevelopment from the 1930s onwards that swept away and renewed much of the Irish Republic's then-run-down but charming capital. It is a fair city that will handsomely repay families visiting for the first time.

Dublin reached its peak as the second city of the British Empire in the late 18th century and retains some of the finest Georgian architecture ever built. If you doubt that, just walk down Henrietta Street to the nearby King's Inns building. But to see the story of Dublin's development at a glance, go to St Stephen's Green and look at the wonderful Georgian house sandwiched between a fancy Victorian building and an uninspiring 1960s office block. The demolition of so much of Georgian Dublin was a serious mistake, with

Ha'penny Bridge

the stunning quality of what remains merely serving to illustrate what has been lost.

The River Liffey divides the city centre into Northside (traditionally working class) and Southside (middle and upper classes), a distinction that has long become blurred. The city is rich in museums and galleries that properly reflect a strong cultural heritage, but the area around the river and the famous O'Connell Bridge summarizes one unarguable truth about modern Dublin. With more than half the

A boat trip along the River Liffey

population under 25, fun-lovers jetting in from all over Europe and a thriving tourist industry, this is a city that simply pulses with energy and life by day and night. Notable areas in this context are Temple Bar with its winding, cobbled thoroughfares and streets around St Stephen's Green, while Grafton Street with its buskers, artists and tourists encapsulates the vibrant character of this 'young' city. But if the sheer exuberance of the place isn't enough, plenty of unique visitor attractions are just waiting to be sampled.

WHEN TO GO:
Any time – the city never sleeps and is popular for weekend breaks, but St Patrick's Day (17 March) is always very special for anyone who has an affinity with Ireland.

TOP FAMILY ATTRACTIONS:
Bang up the kids in atmospheric Kilmainham Gaol, giving dramatic and realistic insight into what is was like to have been confined in this forbidding prison until it closed in 1924 (tours only, very busy in summer); Imaginosity, Dublin's children's museum – a special child-centred creative space for children up to nine years of age and their families; World-famous Dublin Zoo in Phoenix Park (and other attractions in this splendid open space); The Ark, where children aged up to 12 are introduced to the joy, wonder and creativity of the arts; Dublina, a heritage centre that brings Ireland's history from Viking times to life, with hands-on opportunities; Butler's Chocolate Experience – see how it's produced and make your own choccy bear to take home (factory tour, book in advance).

YOU SHOULD KNOW:
Never forget that Dublin was voted 'friendliest city in Europe' in 2007 (still true today!), and of course the Irish always have had a soft spot for the small people.

FOLLOWING PAGES: The 18th-century neoclassical Custom House, located on the north bank of the River Liffey

Madrid

WHEN TO GO:
April, May, June, September and October (high summer is scorching), though the city's charms do justify a trip at any time of year.

TOP FAMILY ATTRACTIONS:
Madrid Zoo & Aquarium in the Casa de Campo park, divided into areas for each continent and containing an impressive array of animals including pandas and koalas, while the aquarium has a dolphin pool; Faunia Parque Biológico de Madrid (Faunia Madrid for short), an imaginative biological creation that is home to over 1,500 different animals from various climates and ecosystems; the sensational CosmoCaixa Science Museum, where both children and adults can learn as they have fun playing; for those who must have some serious action, Madrid has an excellent theme park – Parque de Atracciones (five interesting zones, over 40 rides, special children's area); a 25-km (15-mi) ride out of town to the southeast is another thrill-packed attraction, Parque Warner.

YOU SHOULD KNOW:
Madrid is a sprawling city but getting around is no problem – the Metro de Madrid is one of the most efficient and cheapest urban transport systems in Europe. The ticket machines have instructions in both Spanish and English.

Located on the River Manzanares, Spain's capital is considered to be the main financial, cultural and political centre of the Iberian Peninsula. This wonderful city grew quickly from a little-known 16th-century backwater on the orders of Philip II and boasts some very grand architecture. Despite having a modern infrastructure, Madrid is an atmospheric city that has preserved the character of many historic areas.

Wander through the Puerta del Sol square and see the famous clock whose bells bring in the New Year, or pause for refreshment in the neighbouring Plaza Mayor while imagining both the Spanish Inquisition and bullfighting that once took place within its walls. Also look out for impressive landmarks like the Royal Palace, Teatro Real (Royal Theatre) and the National Library. One highlight every visiting family must be sure to experience is Buen Retiro, once royal gardens and now a

magnificent park featuring beautiful sculptures, monuments, galleries and an attractive lake (hire a boat!). One of Madrid's premier attractions, it hosts free shows and numerous interesting events.

Renowned for its golden triangle of galleries located along the Paseo del Prado, Madrid is the perfect place to introduce youngsters to great art. The triangle comprises the Prado Museum (works by both Velazquez and Goya), the Thyssen Bornemisza Museum (a huge private collection) and the Reina Sofia (great modern art, including Picasso's masterpiece, *Guernica*, famously won back from New York). But the place is not all high culture. Aside from its abundant cultural and historical wealth, Madrid is also famous for its youthful, heady atmosphere, complete with lively pavement cafés and bustling street life. Children have always had a special place in Spanish culture and they are properly catered for nearly everywhere. Madrid is no exception, and makes a great family destination.

The Royal Palace and its beautiful gardens

*The Museum of
Flamenco Dance*

Seville

Despite a hopeful challenge from thrustful Málaga, Seville remains the undisputed capital of southern Spain, bestriding the busy Guadalquivir River as it journeys to the Atlantic. Evidence of Seville's long history is everywhere. Despite the hustle and bustle of a modern city, interested visitors can find powerful reminders of traditionally flamboyant Spanish life in the many *barrios* (old districts) with their narrow streets and charming balconied houses. Seville is the home of flamenco, and this stirring dance form can be seen everywhere.

Along with plenty of all-round attractions, there are enough sights in Seville to satisfy the most compulsive heritage addict. The Romans are represented by various ruins, including an aqueduct. Well-preserved remains at nearby Itálica give a wonderful impression of what Roman Seville (then called Hispalis) must have been like. Moorish influence is also evident, with the Giralda minaret tower being a fine example. Built with sloping ramps to allow the muezzin to ride a horse to the top before calling the faithful to prayer, it was converted to a bell

tower after the Moors were expelled. The 15th-century Seville Cathedral is a vast Gothic triumph that has a stunning, richly gilded interior. Across from the Cathedral is the Alcázar with its beautiful gardens, developed over the centuries from a Moorish palace. Other special monuments include the 16th-century Town Hall and ancient Torre del Oro, a river watchtower. One of the best of Seville's many churches is 13th-century Santa Ana in the Triana district, with an outstanding *reredos*.

A great way to see historic Seville is to hire bikes, though for families who prefer to do it the easy way a leisurely trot around town in a traditional horse-drawn carriage will cover the most important sights. The city also has many fine parks and gardens for unwinding purposes, notably the Maria Luisa Park built for the 1929 Spanish-American World's Fair.

Children riding in a donkey-drawn carriage in the Plaza de España.

FOLLOWING PAGES: The winding walkway on the roof of the Metropol Parasol provides great views.

YOU SHOULD KNOW:
Seville's Holy Week (Semana Santa en Seville) is just before Easter. It's a traditional Spanish festival that is at once both seriously solemn and wonderfully light-hearted. Worth a visit in its own right, quite apart from everything else this great Andalucian city has to offer.

Lisbon

WHEN TO GO:
March to June, September
(unless you have to go during
school holidays and must
brave the summer heat).
TOP FAMILY ATTRACTIONS:
The National Museum of
Ancient Art – located in a
17th-century palace, this is
one of Portugal's most
important museums with a
magnificent collection of fine
art, sculpture, engravings,
jewellery, ceramics, textiles
and furniture; a leisurely Tagus
River sightseeing cruise; the
fabulous Tropical Garden
featuring rare trees and plants
gathered from Portugal's
former colonies; Calouste
Gulbenkian Planetarium for
space-mad kids; the Maritime
Museum in the west wing of
Jerónimos Monastery, evoking
Portugal's past domination of
the seas; Parque das Nações
next to the Tagus estuary, with
attractions dating from the
Expo '98 World Exhibition
including the Oceanarium, one
of the world's biggest
aquariums.
YOU SHOULD KNOW
The oldest exhibit at the
Maritime Museum is a wooden
figure representing the
Archangel Raphael that
accompanied Vasco da Gama
on his historic voyage to India.

*FOLLOWING PAGES: A view
of the Alfama district*

*Walking over the moat
to enter the Castello de
São Jorge.*

On the Atlantic coast where the River Tagus flows into the ocean lies Portugal's capital city of Lisbon (Lisboa), nestled between seven hills. Lisbon is a beautiful, relaxed place full of contrasts, from modern high rises to Art Nouveau buildings, wonderful mosaic pavements, brightly tiled façades and medieval Moorish architecture. The family will find it fascinating and you should allow as much time as possible to sample the city's delights.

Its port has been in constant use for the past three millennia but Lisbon was most powerful between the 15th and 17th centuries, when Portugal was a wealthy nation. Much of this was due to the explorer Vasco da Gama, who discovered a sea route to India in 1498. This led to lively trade in spices and gems, creating great prosperity for Lisbon. In the 17th century gold was discovered in Brazil, bringing in more wealth. However, in 1755 the city was severely damaged by an earthquake and the tsunami that followed. It was never to regain its former prominence.

The oldest district is Alfama, close to the Tagus, which survived almost intact and retains many medieval buildings. Close to the harbour is the Praça do Comercio, one of the most elegant city squares in Europe, surrounded by attractive arcaded buildings. For a view over the city, visit the Castello de São Jorge, a medieval castle built on a hill in the fortified citadel. Probably the most prominent monument in Lisbon and certainly the most successful achievement of the characteristic Manueline style is the magnificent Jerónimos Monastery with its delightful cloister. Close by is the Belem Tower, built in the early 16th century. This defensive yet elegant construction is one of the symbols of the city, a memorial to Portugal's power during the Age of Great Discoveries and a 'must see' for every family on a modern journey of discovery.

Florence

WHEN TO GO:
Spring or autumn (wall-to-wall tourists in summer)
TOP FAMILY ATTRACTIONS:
Forget amusement parks and family fun – soaking up incomparable culture is the name of the game in Florence, with the only problem being to decide what to visit in the time available; the churches of San Miniato al Monte, Santa Maria Novella, Santo Spirito and Orsanmichele; the Museo Galileo science museum, serving as a reminder that art and science were closely related disciplines in medieval times (but don't miss Galileo's severed middle finger!); a picnic in the Boboli Gardens next to the Pitti Palace to enjoy the expansive city views as well as the distinguished collection of sculptures on display.
YOU SHOULD KNOW:
The family must see it, but to avoid frustration book ahead for the Uffizi to avoid that never-ending queue.

Florence is the cultural centre of Italy, perhaps of the Western world, and every family should experience this fabulous city's delights at least once before the kids leave home. Crammed with galleries, wonderful buildings and world-class art treasures, this unspoilt late-medieval city shouts its importance in the cultural and political development of Europe. The architectural jewel of Florence is the Cathedral of Santa Maria del Fiore (Duomo), a Gothic masterpiece containing beautiful frescoes by some of Italy's greatest artists. The Campanile tower and Baptistery buildings are also magical. Both dome and tower are open to visitors and provide excellent views over city rooftops.

At the heart of the city in Piazza della Signoria is the awe-inspiring Fountain of Neptune. This famous marble sculpture lies at the end of a Roman aqueduct, still in working order. A stroll around the city streets will reveal many Renaissance architectural masterpieces, including Brunelleschi's Ospedale degli Innocenti (foundling hospice), the Pazzi chapel in the Church of Santa Croce, Michelangelo's work at San Lorenzo and the Laurentian Library.

Renaissance Florence was dominated by the Medici, the most powerful family in the city from the 15th to the 18th centuries. They patronized many artists and the city's two major galleries house their artworks. The Uffizi has the greatest collection of Italian and Florentine art in the world. On the other side of the River Arno is the Pitti Palace, which contains Medici private works, plus Renaissance masterpieces and a large collection of modern art.

The Arno passes through the centre of Florence, and by wandering along its banks, you can enjoy the unspoiled skyline of domes and towers. Be sure to see the Ponte Vecchio with its built-in houses and shops. Constructed in 1345, this is the only bridge in the city to survive World War II.

FOLLOWING PAGES:
A stunning view of Florence from the top of the Duomo

Tourists outside the marble west façade of the Cathedral of Santa Maria del Fiore, commonly called the Duomo

Verona

Everyone knows the story of Romeo and Juliet (but if it has somehow passed any youngsters by, they'll know all about this tragic tale within two minutes of arriving in Verona). The home city of those star-crossed lovers is strategically located where the River Adage emerges from the Alps onto the Northern Italian plain. It is near Lake Garda on a loop of the fast-flowing river and is a city of bridges (10 of them). Richly endowed with picturesque streets and squares, art and architecture, it is hardly possible to imagine a city that has a more appealing character.

The city's history is well illustrated by famous monuments and buildings. The amphitheatre built around AD 30 is the third largest in Italy and there are other Roman remains, such as a theatre and the rebuilt Gavi Arch. The fourth-century shrine of Verona's patron saint, St Zeno, lies beneath the stunning Basilica of San Zeno Maggiore, a triumph of Romanesque architecture built in the 12th century. Other Romanesque masterpieces include the small Basilica of San Lorenzo, the large Church of Santa Maria Antica and the striking Cathedral, with its fine Gothic interior. Indeed, there are so many fascinating churches in

WHEN TO GO:
Any time, although Verona gets very crowded in summer so June and September are good months for those who like breathing space.

TOP FAMILY ATTRACTIONS:
The Natural History Museum, with its exceptional collection of fossils; Castelvecchio Museum in a 14th-century castle, with superb sculptures, statues and paintings...plus a great view of the city's terracotta roofscape from the top of the keep; sweeping views from the Torre dei Lamberti (lift for parents, stairs for kids!); Juliet's (Capulet) and Romeo's (Montague) houses (the former in a courtyard off Via Capello featuring a wonderful old stone balcony falsely claiming association with the fictional lovers); Il Museo Del Giocatto, an exciting museum of childhood in the Verona hills featuring (among other things) an astonishing toy collection; a trip out of town to Gardaland, one of Europe's most popular amusement parks, where rides include the fearsome Raptor.

YOU SHOULD KNOW:
Squeamish families should have a care when sampling anything billed as 'traditional food of Verona', for this description definitely includes meals featuring horse or donkey meat.

The view from the Torre dei Lamberti looking down into Piazza del Erbe.

RIGHT: The Roman Arena

Frescoes in the Pisanello Room, Museo di Castelvecchio

Verona that a month could be spent appreciating them all.

The old town's central feature is the elongated Piazza del Erbe, once the Roman forum and now the scene of a lively market. This must surely be one of the most delightful old squares in Italy. Nearby Piazza dei Signori is surrounded by palaces, including one now serving as the Town Hall. The Loggia del Consiglio is one of the finest early Renaissance buildings in the country, crowned by statues of famous Veronans. The city walls are a 15th-century architectural statement, built to serve both a defensive and aesthetic function – marvel at the superb Porta del Palio.

Corfu (Kérkyra)

*Aqualand Water Park,
Agios Ioannis*

Corfu is the largest and northernmost of the beautiful,
lush Ionian Islands and is a superb (and therefore
popular) destination for family holidays in the sun. It
lies off the Albanian coast at the entrance to the
Adriatic Sea. Corfu Town, its elegant capital city, is
built on a peninsula on the east coast. It's an
authentic, fortified Mediterranean port, enclosed by
two magnificent Venetian citadels. Throughout its
long history Corfu has been a renowned cultural
centre for the arts, literature and music – a tradition
that still thrives today. For hundreds of years it was a
major trading centre under the rule of Venice, then
briefly France. The city is renowned for wonderful
Venetian and (surprisingly) British neo-classical
architecture – it was actually British territory in the
19th century before being ceded to Greece in 1864.

Formal gardens and the Palace of St Michael and St George, built in 1819.

(There is still an active cricket club!)

The Spianáda is a huge central square, which has at its northern end the fine 19th-century British Residency, later used as a palace by the Greek royal family. Along one side there is the Listón, a lovely French-built arcaded street lined with cafés. But the real character of this historic city is to be found in the Kantounia – a labyrinth of narrow cobble-stoned lanes – where you will find the city's best architecture and where there is an almost magical surprise round every corner. Do not miss what remains of the old Jewish quarter, the ancient Campiello district and Kofineta, the area behind the Spianáda.

Corfu Town exudes an air of Italian rather than Greek culture and has a unique flavour. It is one of the most charming island cities to be found anywhere, with a character and history that cannot fail to seduce visitors who abandon their holiday beaches to explore its atmospheric delights, or make it their base on the island.

park with assorted adventures for older kids and plenty of gentler activities for little ones (open mid May to October); a day trip to Paleokastritsa, grandly billed as 'the island's most treasured beauty spot' (lovely beaches!).

YOU SHOULD KNOW:
Corfu has a long history of hospitality to foreign incomers and visitors, as recorded in the 20th century in Gerald Durrell's reminiscence My Family and Other Animals, about childhood years spent living in Corfu during the 1930s. Prince Philip, Duke of Edinburgh and husband of Queen Elizabeth II, was born at Mon Repos, The Royal Estate on Corfu (can be visited).

Antalya

WHEN TO GO:
Any time of year, as there is no real winter here. Very crowded, extremely hot and noisy in high summer.
TOP FAMILY ATTRACTIONS:
Antalya Museum, featuring interesting items from various different historical eras that were found locally – if you only do one cultural activity, make it this one; panoramic views from Hidirlik Tower in Karaoglu Park; swimming with dolphins at Dolphinland; Antalya Aquapark – if bathing in the azure sea isn't enough, this is the place for all the fun of the flumes, slides and other water-park adventures (suitable for young children too).
YOU SHOULD KNOW:
The skiing season in the Taurus Mountains is from November to May so sporty families who time their visit right can go skiing in the morning and swim in the Med that afternoon. Every October there is the Film Festival – the largest in Turkey.

In only 30 years the run-down fishing town of Antalya has transformed itself into the vibrant capital of Turkey's Mediterranean coast, becoming the cultural and tourist centre of southern Turkey. In the summer this pleasant city accommodates up to two million visitors, attracting them with lively nightlife, superb shopping and miles of beaches together with a picturesque old quarter, plenty of cultural sites and events in and around the city.

A major part of the charm of Antalya is its spectacular setting. It is built on travertine cliff terraces overlooking the sea, with the snow-capped Taurus Mountains as a backdrop. The symbol of the city is Yivli Minare – a 38-m (125-ft) high, 13th-century tiled minaret – reaching up into the sky from the picturesque lanes of the historic Kaleiçi district full of old Greek, Italian and Turkish buildings. The cobbled streets wind down the cliff to the city's ancient Roman harbour and the 19th-century Iskele Mosque, built over a natural spring, plus an award-winning marina.

Despite the inevitable concrete blocks, the modern part of the city has pleasant boulevards fringed with palm trees, expensive shopping streets including Isiklar, Ataturk and Cumhuriyet, also the amazing Konyaalti pebble beach that extends miles to the west, backed by an attractive cliff-top promenade of hotels, shops and restaurants with all sorts of entertainment and activities. A short way off to the east is Lara beach – miles of sand, becoming progressively more deserted the further you walk. There are wonderful views of the mountains in the distance, while close by there are beautiful landscapes and fascinating archaeological sites. Antalya is an almost perfect destination for a family holiday, combining the cultural and entertainment attractions of a city with the pleasures of a beach holiday.

Tekeli Memet Pasa Mosque, in the historic district of Kaleiçi

Ride the funicular railway between the two halves of town.

Zagreb

On the Sava River near the southern slopes of Mount Medvednica lies the Croatian capital of Zagreb, a glorious Austro-Hungarian city full of lovely churches, museums and art galleries. Once two towns, the city is divided into upper and lower areas, each with its own distinctive character. The two halves are separated by a vast main square, Trg Bana Jelacica. It's an excellent

destination for families keen to see something different and get a flavour of the historic Balkans.

With its winding cobbled streets the upper town, Gornji Grad, is the oldest part of the city. It is set on two hills and boasts a wide array of lovely buildings, as well as the city's main market. Built in 1217 but remodelled over the years, the Cathedral has a stately neo-Gothic façade and twin steeples which were added in the 1880s. Inside it is breathtaking. The north wall features the Ten Commandments written in 12th-century script.

Zagreb's lower town is a place of elegant squares, gardens, wide boulevards and parks. Donji Grad was built to a grid design in the late 19th century and is home to most of Zagreb's numerous museums. These reflect the history, art and culture not only of Zagreb and Croatia, but also the rest of the world. The Archaeological Museum's most famous exhibits are the Egyptian collection, the Zagreb mummy and the oldest Etruscan inscription in the world. The Croatian Natural History Museum holds an extensive collection of Neanderthal remains, while the Museum of the City of Zagreb deals with cultural, artistic, economic and political history from Roman times to the present day. There are other museums, but also plenty of more light-hearted activities for the family to enjoy should culture fatigue set in.

WHEN TO GO:
March to October

TOP FAMILY ATTRACTIONS:
A trip out of town to Medvedgrad Castle on the slopes of Medvednica mountain, high above Zagreb, for a spectacular view of the city; Riding the funicular railway between the two halves of town; Maksimir Park – designed in 1784, this is the biggest park in southeast Europe and is home to an old oak forest, sunny open spaces, romantic lakes, varied wildlife – plus Zagreb Zoo, an excellent facility which is located in the southern part of the park; the Jarun sports and leisure centre, featuring a lake where people can row, paddle, sail, surf, swim, jog, bike, roller skate, and skateboard; Zagreb Karting Centre for some fast and furious action.

YOU SHOULD KNOW:
The Lotrscak Tower, built in the 13th century to protect the city gates, affords wonderful views over the city. But don't jump if you hear an unexpected explosion at midday. By long tradition, a cannon is fired from the top of the tower at noon.

Ljubljana

WHEN TO GO:
June to September for festivals of music, theatre and art.
TOP FAMILY ATTRACTIONS:
Ljubljana Castle – the city's most spectacular sight, and repository of every stage of its history in the different buildings within the complex; the 'Summer in Old Town' Festival of (mostly) free classical music concerts in the loveliest churches, inner courtyards and squares – a great way to discover them; Tivoli Park for grand avenues, fine buildings (and a children's playground); the House of Experiments for entertaining learning with over 40 interactive scientific challenges; a small but appealing Zoo (guided tours and workshops at weekends); Atlantis aqua park, one of the biggest indoor water parks in Europe.
YOU SHOULD KNOW:
Ljubljana looks even better from a hot-air balloon – it's the family experience of a lifetime (at a price!).

If perceptions prickle with déja-vu and a quick check of all five senses registers total satisfaction, and on top of that an adrenalin surge warns you that something utterly surprising and wonderful is going to happen – you're almost certainly in Ljubljana for the first time. It is a successful blend of the best of old and new; of small-town friendly with imposingly formal; of architectural beauty and ruthlessly modern function. Small for a city, it punches well above its weight in ambience, looks, treasures to behold and things for the family to do.

The city owes its architectural beauty to two earthquakes. The first, in 1511, destroyed most of medieval Laibach, its name as the capital of the Austrian Habsburg Duchy of Carniola. The city handpicked the finest Italian architects to create the façades, arched courtyards and ornate staircases for the magnificent churches, palaces and public and private buildings on show today. One of many masterpieces is Venetian sculptor Francesco Robba's *Fountain of Carniolan Rivers* (1751) in front of the Renaissance Town Hall.

The Napoleonic wars brought a stylistic interregnum, but a second earthquake in 1895 created a golden opportunity for the city to employ its native son, Joze Plecnik – a man who had just restyled parts of Prague and Vienna as bywords for modern grace. From 1921, Plecnik composed the new Ljubljana in Neo-Classicist and Secessionist (Austrian Art Nouveau) styles. Whole sections of the city, churches, markets, and even bridges, are testament to his inventive genius. Don't miss the famous Dragon Bridge.

Ljubljana's other secret is its youth and energy, shared by every age group, and every sector. Summer is a non-stop festival of music and theatre of every kind and the streets of the Old Town, where willows droop over the riverside café terraces, bubble with the happy, cosmopolitan buzz of Europe's most elegant small city.

Take a cruise along the river and admire the many architectural styles in the city.

Brno

The capital of Moravia and the Czech Republic's second city, Brno is proud of its history, but prouder still of its present. Culture vultures looking for a historical fix will get it in spades from this former stronghold of the medieval Prmyslid dynasty, which twice saw off besieging Hussites (1428 and 1430), Swedes (1643 and 1645) and finally, after rebuilding as a Baroque fortress, Prussians in 1742. With nothing left to prove, but a superb collection of churches, monasteries, palaces, squares, markets and monuments still magnificently extant to prove it with, Brno returned to what it did and does best – industry and commerce. Culture was to be pursued only in tandem with progress.

As a civic philosophy it's hugely successful, and Brno established its Exhibition Centre as long ago as 1928 and nurtured its growth (despite Nazis and Communists) to the current annual statistics of 40 trade fairs and one million visitors. But for families interested only in a stimulating and entertaining visit, there's also plenty on offer. The city appreciates motor racing, so after years gauging what it can do and what people enjoy, hosts regular car and motorcycle events at the highest international levels. On top of that, just for fun, every June it hosts Ignis Brunensis – not a show, but an international fireworks competition which attracts 200,000 people. It makes September's wine festival look positively traditional, except that the city is surrounded by vineyards and nobody is likely to leave empty-handed.

You have to love a city that thinks so positively and comes up with the active and/or interactive goods. Brno's unofficial symbol is the former Bauhaus Director Mies van der Rohe's Tugendhat Villa in the town, listed recently by UNESCO as a masterpiece of functionalism. It's perfect – visitors know that Brno will do everything possible to help them enjoy themselves.

WHEN TO GO:
Year-round – there is always a fair, festival or major event going on.
TOP FAMILY ATTRACTIONS:
The spectacular view from the 63-m (207-ft) high tower (built 1240) of the Old Town Hall; a gruesome torture chamber at imposing Spilberk Castle, on the hill overlooking Brno; the city zoo (small but with more than 500 mammals, reptiles, birds and amphibians, including creatures from every continent except Antarctica); Brno Observatory and Planetarium, exploring the Universe and science generally in an understandable and entertaining way, with some interaction.
YOU SHOULD KNOW:
When you hear the Petrov Cathedral bells tolling noon at 11.00, don't reset your watch. It's an old tradition dating back to the Swedish siege of 1645.

The Cathedral of St Peter and Paul dominates Brno's skyline.

Prague

Prague has been the political, cultural, and economic centre of the Czech state for over 1,000 years. Lying on a bend in the River Vltava, half-way between Berlin and Vienna, it is set on seven hills topped by lovely castles and churches. Prague is one of the most beautiful cities in Europe. In 1993, after the split of Czechoslovakia, Prague became the capital of the new Czech Republic and has become one of the most visited cities in Europe, famous for its café culture and vibrant street life in lovely surroundings. No family that pays a visit will be disappointed.

The city's heyday was during the 14th century and the reign of Charles IV. He rebuilt Prague Castle and Vysehrad, and erected imposing Charles Bridge. Many new churches were built, including St Vitus'

Cathedral, and Charles was crowned as Holy Roman Emperor. He wanted Prague to be one of the most beautiful cities in the world, dominating the whole empire, with Prague Castle dominating the city and the gothic Cathedral dominating the castle. To this end, he created many beautiful buildings which are still with us today.

The castle has remained the seat of power. One of the largest castles in the world, it houses the crown jewels of the Bohemian Kingdom. Nearby is the 18th-century Sternberg Palace, home to the National Gallery with its superb collection of Old Masters. The complex also contains the wonderful Royal Gardens and the stately gothic St Vitus' Cathedral, begun in 1344. The walls of the chapel that houses the tomb of St Wenceslas are lined with precious stones and beautiful paintings.

Prague's old town is an atmospheric area of cobbled streets, alleyways, superb churches and palaces. The Little Quarter (Malá Strana) lies below the castle walls and is also well worth exploring.

1891 for the Jubilee Exhibition – sensational panoramas plus observatory and hall of mirrors; the National Marionette Theatre, a world centre for puppetry, plus the fascinating Marionette Museum; Sea World aquarium (15 minutes from the town centre by tram).
YOU SHOULD KNOW: Entrance fees are payable at most tourist attractions.

LEFT: The opera Don Giovanni with Marionettes

ABOVE: The Old Town Hall is famous for its astronomical clock.

There are quirky statues everywhere!

Bratislava

Throughout the Soviet era, Bratislava was dismissed as the drab, industrialized second city of Czechoslovakia. Even its historic Old Town was as tatty as the pollution-stained suburbs spreading in every direction. Well, adventurous families who ignore this old reputation and see for themselves are in for a nice surprise. Since 1990, few places can have done more, more successfully, to reclaim their past – and nowhere else has officialdom combined determined regeneration with irrepressible glee and a genuinely amusing sense of humour. Bratislava, restored as capital of an independent Slovakia, is bursting with life.

Once the frontier of the Roman Empire, it was called Pressburg when its strategic importance on the Danube was recognized with heavy fortifications in the 12th century. By 1536, with the Turks in Budapest, Bratislava was confirmed as the Hungarian capital, hosting 19 imperial coronations in the next 300 years. By then the Old Town and environs were packed with castles, palaces, spires and churches, and it was in the

Mirror Hall of the Primate's Palace that Napoleon signed the Peace of Bratislava after the Battle of Austerlitz in 1805.

This is the kind of history that Bratislava is revitalizing, with pedestrian precincts and a policy of encouraging street cafés and bars, so the city's historic heart is now ablaze with light, music, street theatre and strolling couples.

Join the tourist train for a tour of the Old Town.

There are quirky statues everywhere – like the Napoleonic soldier leaning over your shoulder as you sit on a bench or the grinning, helmeted man emerging from a manhole (Why? Find the oddball answer for yourself!) or an old gentleman doffing his top hat to the sky (commemorating a man who lost his mind after the deportation of his Jewish fiancée by the Nazis). History in Bratislava certainly has human empathy, and human scale. The city doesn't compete with other European capitals for tourist business. It is far too busy and entertaining being itself.

Budapest

*The Hungarian
Parliament Building*

Known as 'the Pearl of the Danube', Budapest is made up of three distinct towns: Óbuda and Buda (the historic medieval city on Castle Hill) on the west bank of the River Danube and Pest (the administrative and commercial city) on the east. In 1873 the three towns merged and today large areas of architectural, archaeological and cultural importance are listed as a UNESCO World Heritage Site.

The heart of Budapest around the Castle Hill area is beautiful, despite suffering many invasions. The city was badly damaged during a siege at the end of World War II, when attacking Russians fought with defending German and Hungarian troops. The Hungarians, however, have always rebuilt their city and today it is as lovely as ever.

Buda Castle is the historical seat of Hungarian kings and today houses the Historical Museum of Budapest. It displays marvellous paintings, including

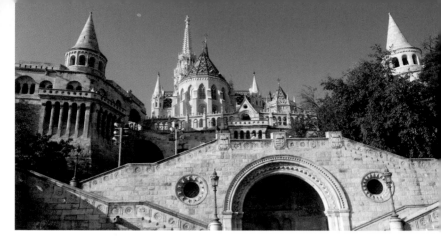

Buda Castle

those of Eastern European and Hungarian artists alongside modern greats such as Picasso and Lichtenstein. Nearby, the neo-gothic Mathias Church has a colourful roof and a wonderful interior, renovated back to its 13th-century splendour. In Pest, visiting families should be sure to explore the National Museum dedicated to the history and ecology of the country. St Stephen's Basilica, with its neo-Renaissance dome, offers 360-degree views of the city for those with a head for heights. The National Opera House is spectacularly ornate, built during the glory days of the Austro-Hungarian Empire, while the Parliament building is also worth seeing (the Hungarian crown jewels are on display there).

If the kids tire of cultural sightseeing, visit the Danube island of Margit-sziget, a popular recreational area for tourists and locals alike. Another island in the Danube, Óbudai-sziget, hosts one of Europe's largest music and cultural events every August, the Sziget Festival.

The Funicular Railway is a great way to climb Castle Hill!

Gdańsk

WHEN TO GO:
April to October
TOP FAMILY ATTRACTIONS:
The Town Hall – a stunning building that now houses a museum charting the formation and history of the city; Gdańsk's zoological gardens, in a lovely setting with over 200 different species of animals, many endangered (plus mini-zoo for the younger generation); the Maritime Museum at the old port, featuring Poland's great seafaring traditions; a short trip up the coast to Gdynia Aquarium with its 1,500

Situated on the Baltic Sea in the north of Poland, Gdańsk (Danzig in German) is a beautiful port city with a long history. Its fort was built in the 10th century by Mieszko I of Poland as defence against pagans, but in 1308 it was seized and demolished by the Teutonic Knights. The city prospered under the control of the Knights and became a member of the Hanseatic League, a trading alliance. By the middle of the 16th century it was the most important Baltic port and Poland's largest city.

This former power and wealth is soon obvious to interested visitors – buildings are bigger and streets broader than in other medieval cities. Gdańsk has many

fine structures from the time of the Hanseatic League. Most attractions are located near Long Street and Long Market, a pedestrian area known as Royal Road. The Golden Gate is one of the most notable. It was designed by architect Abraham van den Blocke in 1612-14 to replace a 13th-century Gothic gate and forms a part of the old city fortifications. Next to it is the late-Gothic building of the Brotherhood of St George.

St Mary's Church is possibly the largest brick church in the world. Started in 1379, it is an aisled hall church with a transept that can accommodate up to 25,000 worshippers.

Dlugi Targ is the beautiful main square. Nearby is the 14th-century town hall and other architectural gems, including the unique 17th-century houses of St Mary's Street. Take time to stroll through old streets and along the river banks of the ancient port. It was here that World War II started in 1939, when the German battleship *Schleswig-Holstein* attacked the naval fort at Westerplatte. Much of the city was devastated during the war, but almost all of its historic centre has been painstakingly restored.

marine occupants; the adjoining seaside town of Sopot – a 25-minute train journey from the city, this is Poland's premier beach resort, an entertaining destination with luxury shops, cafés and other assorted amusements.

YOU SHOULD KNOW:
The Gdańsk tourist card grants the user free entrance to museums, free use of public transport (including trams, trolleybuses, buses and the SKM commuter train), plus additional perks including good discounts at over 200 venues.

ABOVE: The old port

LEFT: Rooftops of Główne Miasto (old town) from the tower of the historic Town Hall

The Cathedral of the Assumption of the Virgin

Varna

The memorial to the Battle of Varna in 1444 looks like a single-storey outhouse with a classical façade. Set into an ancient Thracian burial-mound on the edge of a Black Sea beach, it hardly does justice to the last major battle of the Crusades – one that led to the subsequent fall of Constantinople in 1453 and subjugation of half Europe by the Ottoman Turks.

Varna may not have a sense of proportion, but it does have space. Many civilizations have passed this way, leaving a cultural kaleidoscope of colour and fine workmanship. All of them wanted a place in the sun on a grand scale. Varna is full of glorious architecture like the Dormition of the Theotokos Cathedral, the Roman baths and Euxinograd Palace, but the Ottoman city of wooden houses and narrow alleys hardly survives. After 1878, an emerging Bulgarian middle class built comfortable neoclassical, Art Deco and Art Nouveau homes in their place. The medieval city walls were recycled into the neo-Byzantine Cathedral, new boulevards and elegant mansions. Even so, Varna is crammed with places to ogle and admire, still with large gardens in between.

Varna's carefree sense of taking pleasure where you can has always included rich and poor. It still does, and the advent of modern tourism facilities makes it better for everyone, to the point where it has become a great destination for a family holiday. The space still exists for opulent new villas and exclusive enclaves and the skyline both in the centre and on the beach shows how fast new money is arriving. Only the roads pose a threat to the city's traditional greenery. Varna is on the cusp of yet another re-invention as a beguiling resort and the signs are positive that the city will continue to grow without losing its long tradition of fun and laughter to either regulation or resort snobbism.

WHEN TO GO:
April to October for the best weather, although October to March is both feasible and quieter.
TOP FAMILY ATTRACTIONS:
The oldest gold treasure hoard in the world at the Archaeological Museum; the Sea Garden – a complex of attractions including Cosmonauts' Alley, Aquarium, Museum of Natural History and children's corner; the Nicolaus Copernicus National Observatory and Planetarium, the biggest and most modern planetarium in the Balkans; exploring the amazing petrified forest to the west of town; a show at the Festa Dolphinarium (great for kids); Rappongi Beach with its (artificial) palm trees and super sands; for bold family members only, bungee-jumping from the 50-m (164-ft) high Asparuhov Bridge.
YOU SHOULD KNOW:
Be aware that taxi drivers in Varna often charge way over the odds (up to 10 times the right price) – to check for the correct fare per kilometre look at the small square sticker located on the rear windows.

Part of the gold treasure hoard on show at the Archaeological Museum

WHEN TO GO:
April to October
TOP FAMILY ATTRACTIONS:
The fascinating Folk Art
Museum, with over 15,000
exhibits (folk costumes,
jewellery, interiors of
traditional peasant homes and
much more); the panorama of
the harbour from the

*Piata Ovidiu, the
central square of
Constanta's old quarter*

Constanta

Originally a Greek colony – 6th-century BC Tomis –
850 years later it was renamed by the Roman
Emperor Constantine the Great after his half-sister
Constantiana. Ottomans shortened that to Constanta
during its most prosperous era between the 13th and
15th centuries, but eventually the city declined under
Turkish rule. It was revived as a port and resort by
King Carol I of Romania
and during the 19th
century gained the
elegant mansions and
hotels which first made it
internationally famous. It
grew to its present
ranking as fourth-biggest
port in Europe without
threatening the endless
stretches of white, sandy
beaches on which
tourism depends, and
leads a successful double
life as industrial leader
and holiday magnet.

Constanta's old
centre and original
harbour reveal the
durability of its success.
Piata Ovidiu (Ovidiu's
Square), dedicated in
1887 to the poet Ovid,
exiled here by the
Emperor Augustus in the
year AD 8, is built round
the remains of a colossal
Roman complex on three
levels that once linked

the upper town to the harbour. Developed continuously from the 4th to 7th centuries, you can still see how the workshops, warehouses and shops inter-related, and visit the nearby baths and aqueduct. The greatest treasure of all is one of the world's longest mosaic pavements.

You'll see ruins everywhere, with the rest of Constanta's history arranged around them. Besides encouraging the boulevards and avenues, King Carol built mosques and churches as practical gifts to beautify the resort. The Art Nouveau Casino's sumptuous architecture came later in the early 1920s; and the pedestrian area surrounding it, with its bars and cafés, is still Constanta's favourite evening promenade, with the best view. Constanta may not be electric with action, but it's beautiful, civilized, and absorbing. It takes a long history to create such a relaxed atmosphere.

Romanian Navy Museum, which has exhibits like Greek triremes and a 17th-century Venetian celestial globe; a trip out to Mamaia, 5 km (3 mi) north of the old centre, with some of the best beaches, friendliest people and assorted attractions including a water park; Satul de Vacanta amusement park featuring rides, a bowling alley and open-air market (between Constanta and Mamaia).

YOU SHOULD KNOW:
The Constanta Aquarium holds 60 species of fish from the Black Sea and the Danube Delta. Local restaurants will serve you most of them, including sturgeon. Legend has it that Jason landed here with the Argonauts after finding the Golden Fleece.

Detail of Piata Ovidiu's mosaic pavement

Moscow ✓

WHEN TO GO:
Year round, although April–June and September–November are the most comfortable months and winters call for fur hats.

TOP FAMILY ATTRACTIONS:
Famous sights galore – awesome Red Square, the Kremlin, St Basil's Cathedral, the glorious celebration of Ivan the Terrible's victory at Kazan, Lenin's tomb, the nearby Bolshoi Theatre and so many more; Pushkin Museum of Fine Arts containing Russia's second-best art collection; a ride on the Metro to appreciate the fabulous decorative variety

Moscow is one of a handful of world cities that might be called truly enigmatic. The harder you try to capture its essence, the more it eludes you. You can't really separate its rich history from its daily role in writing the future: as the capital and barometer of such an influential country, Moscow is both dictator and victim of events. This contradiction at the heart of its character is what provokes such strong responses in its visitors, who (old or young) cannot help but be energized by this stimulating capital city.

You only have to stand in Red Square to feel the shocking difference between familiar images and actuality. The Kremlin and St Basil's Cathedral radiate an aura of power, creating both exhilaration and discomfort. Even their beauty is manipulative. In this single place, Moscow draws together threads of church and state in a demonstration aimed at over-awing citizen and visitor alike.

Moscow hasn't always felt like this. It wasn't mentioned anywhere until 1147, although it rapidly assumed a central role in Russian affairs. For many years the city paid homage to Batu, Genghis Khan's

LEFT: Cathedral Square in the Kremlin

RIGHT: St Basil's Cathedral

of its 'underground palaces' (stations to the unimaginative); Gorky Park with children's play areas, fun fairs, amusement rides and 'the Cosmic Experience' to thrill space-mad kids; the Bolshoi Circus, featuring trapeze and acrobatics; the Grand Planetarium for daytime star-gazing.

YOU SHOULD KNOW:
Two interesting anomalies can be found inside the Kremlin walls – the massive Tsar Bell and the huge Tsar Cannon. The former was never rung (Russia's largest bell crashed down after a fire in 1737 and broke). The latter was never fired (cast in 1586 to defend the Kremlin, but deemed too decorative and precious to use).

RIGHT AND BELOW: Art on display in the Metro

grandson and leader of the Golden Horde. The early Tsars had to co-exist with unruly Boyars until Ivan IV (The Terrible) finally made Moscow the seat of all real power in his expanding Russian state.

Although the classical European city of St Petersburg remained Russia's capital from 1712 until the 1917 revolution both Napoleon and Hitler targeted Moscow, a cultural amalgam of Asian steppe, Cossack marsh and tribal Rus. But Muscovites rebuilt it quickly whenever it burned, because then as now their city inspired passion. You can see the scars, and you can palpably feel Moscow's and Mother Russia's soul. Now the place is on the cusp of another era – unfettered capitalism *á la Russe* – and the city seethes. In all its history, there's never been a better time to visit.

St Petersburg

WHEN TO GO:
May to July
TOP FAMILY ATTRACTIONS:
The State Hermitage one of
the biggest and best museums
in the world, with sumptuous
contents housed in six historic
buildings (including the Winter
Palace) along Palace
Embankment; the State
Russian Museum, home to the
world's largest collection of
Russian fine art; a railway
museum at the old Warsaw
Station (a must-experience
attraction for children and
those with an interest in
trains!); Pavlovsk Park with an
aviary, charming foot bridges,
trails, ponds, gardens and a
palace that belonged to Paul I;
the Rasputin Museum in

*A carriage stands
outside the State
Hermitage Museum.*

St Petersburg was founded by Tsar Peter the Great in 1703
as the capital of the Russian Empire, and remained so for
more than two centuries until the revolution of 1917. This is
a stunningly beautiful place with a rich history, offering
many treats for lovers of art and architecture and providing
a must-visit destination for families who like to tick off the
world's great cities (and can live without amusement parks).

Tsar Peter named it after his patron saint, the apostle
Saint Peter, and chose a site on the delta of the Neva River.
The Neva, with its many canals and their granite
embankments and bridges, sets St Petersburg apart from
other Russian cities. Dominated by the Baroque Winter
Palace along the river front, it is imbued with Russian
imperial history. Commissioned by Tsarina Elizabeth, the
lavish interior of the palace reflects the opulent lives of the
tsars. Catherine the Great added the Hermitage in 1764 to

house her large art collection.

The main street is Nevsky Prospekt, which offers many rewarding sights. These include the Rastrelliesque Stroganov Palace, a monument to Catherine the Great, the Art Nouveau Bookhouse, the Anichkov Bridge with its remarkable horse statues, churches, an enormous 18th-century shopping centre, a 19th-century department store and the Russian National Library.

There are dozens of baroque and neoclassical palaces in the city, plus an astonishing array of churches. St Isaac's Cathedral has an enormous dome covered with gold, while the Cathedral of Peter and Paul in Palace Square contains the tombs of Peter the Great and his successors. The huge neoclassical Kazan Cathedral is modelled on St Peter's in Rome. The Alexander Nevsky Monastery comprises two cathedrals and five churches in various styles. It is also known for its cemetery, with the graves of many well-known figures, such as Dostoyevsky, Krylov, Ilyich, Tchaikovsky and Mussorgsky. So much to see!

Visitors admire the stunning interior of the State Hermitage Museum.

Yusupov's Palace, one of St Petersburg's most beautiful buildings (dedicated to Russia's most scandalous figure in the place where he was murdered).

YOU SHOULD KNOW:
The very first house in St Petersburg was a small, wooden cabin that Peter the Great inhabited for five years, and it is now filled with some of his original belongings. Due to adverse weather and geographical conditions, there was a high mortality rate among workers creating his new city, so Peter levied a yearly conscription of 40,000 peasants from all parts of the country. Half of them died or escaped on the long trek to the giant building site.

127

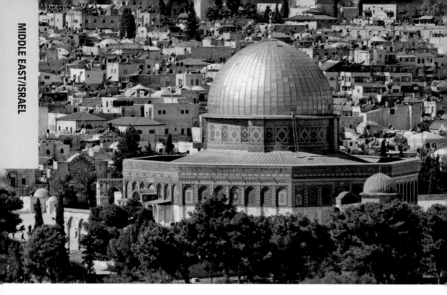

*The Dome of the Rock,
Temple Mount*

Jerusalem

WHEN TO GO:
March, April or September to
November.
TOP FAMILY ATTRACTIONS:
The city's hallowed religious
sites, notably Temple Mount,
the Dome of the Rock, al-Aqsa
Mosque, Church of the Holy
Sepulchre, Wailing Wall;
Hezekiah's tunnel and
Ramparts Walk for historical
insight into the Old City; the
YMCA Tower for fantastic
views (restricted to four
people at a time); Bloomfield
Science Museum for
interactive learning that's fun;
The Biblical Zoo (officially the
Tisch Family Zoological
Gardens) containing animals

Jerusalem is many things to many people, but nobody
can deny that it has an epic history. Set in the Judean
mountains between the Mediterranean and the Dead
Sea, many different powers have fought for, ruled
over and lost Jerusalem over the centuries. It has
been the spiritual centre of the Jewish people since
the 10th century, and Jerusalem is now the capital of
modern Israel. But it also contains major Christian
sites and is the third-holiest city in Islam.

The walled Old City lies at its centre, with Jewish
West Jerusalem on one side and Arab East Jerusalem
on the other. The Temple Mount and its Wailing Wall
is of huge significance for Jews, the Church of the
Holy Sepulchre is where Christ is said to have been
crucified and the Dome of the Rock and al-Aqsa

Mosque has critical importance for Muslims (Muhammad is said to have ascended to heaven from Temple Mount). In fact, there are too many historic attractions and sites in Old Jerusalem to list.

It was on the highly contested Temple Mount that Abraham is said to have prepared his son for sacrifice. The First and Second Temples were built on the site to be the repository of the Ark of the Covenant. The only remaining wall of the Second Holy Temple, known as the Western or Wailing Wall, marks the border between Temple Mount and the Jewish quarter. Here Jews pray out loud, or push written prayers into the cracks between the ancient stones. The gilded Dome of the Rock stands in the temple compound with the Al-Aqsa Mosque. Bordering Temple Mount is the Muslim quarter, entered through the main Damascus Gate. Rich in architecture from the Mamaluk period (1250–1516), the Muslim souk with its winding alleyways, is a great place to explore.

native to Israel mentioned in the Bible; the Botanical gardens (with miniature train for the kids); the truly amazing Time Elevator, presenting three millennia of Jerusalem's history with special effects; Liberty Bell Park, complete with puppet theatre.

YOU SHOULD KNOW: Because of perennial security measures, crossing between different areas of the city can take time and be a real hassle.

Children entering a building that resembles Noah's Ark at the Biblical Zoo in West Jerusalem.

Dubai City

Every family's wish list must surely include a visit to hedonistic Dubai in the Arabian Peninsula. This is the second-largest developing city in the world after Shanghai, attracting 800 new residents a day – a cultural melting pot of over 70 nationalities. Dubai was a pearl trading centre until the 1930s, when it went into decline until the discovery of oil in the 1960s led to a sudden resurgence.

Today, the booming city has become a byword for luxury living – a base for international businesses and a hideaway for celebrities, rock stars and shadowy millionaires drawn by an epicurean lifestyle, set against a wonderful backdrop of sandy beaches and desert landscapes. Dubai City is a delightful playground for the western tourist, providing every conceivable form of leisure activity. Palm Jumeirah is an ambitious development of man-made islands, each in the shape of a palm tree with a trunk, crown and

*A camel and Bedouin
tent outside Bastakia,
the old quarter*

RIGHT: Wild Wadi
Water Park

fronds, all enclosed by a crescent breakwater, with luxury hotels, private mansions, prestige apartments, restaurants, entertainment and diving sites. This massive development can be seen from space.

Despite Dubai's headlong gallop into the 21st century, an interesting and attractive old quarter remains. Bastakia is reached by *abra* (water taxi) and visitors will discover an area of narrow lanes with a distinctly 'Arabian Nights' charm. The ornate late 19th-century courtyard houses were originally the homes of Persian pearl and textile dealers. In dramatic contrast, the Burj Khalifa on Sheikh Zayed Road is a gleaming post-modern tower set in an artificial lake, snatching the crown as the world's tallest building. Dubai has breathtaking modern architecture, beautiful beaches and a sophisticated entertainment industry. The city revels unashamedly in an air of conspicuous consumption – a triumph for hedonistic capitalism that seems (almost) immune to economic downturn.

LEFT: Building sandcastles on Jumeirah Beach.

Dubai Aquarium and Underwater Zoo, part of the Dubai Mall

133

ASIA

Karachi

WHEN TO GO:
November to February are the most pleasant months but even in high summer the sea breezes help to relieve the worst of the heat.
TOP FAMILY ATTRACTIONS:
Mohatta Palace – a museum that was originally a magnificent private summer residence; Karachi Zoo, long-established with a wonderful Elephant House; Safari Park (zoo, children's playgrounds and Go-Aish Adventure Park); Aladdin Park (amusement park, adjacent water park and huge shopping mall); Sinbad Amusement Park for breath-taking rides; The Great Fiesta Water Park, Asia's biggest; fabulous beaches on the Arabian Sea, with associated water sports.
YOU SHOULD KNOW:
Although it has a larger middle class than any other city in Pakistan, there is still a distressing disparity between rich and poor here which will provide youngsters with an unforgettable insight into the realities of Third World life.

It is hard to believe that fewer than 200 years ago this sprawling megacity was a fishing village known as Kolachi. The British saw its potential and rapidly developed it as an international port. By 1876 it had become the thriving city of Karachi with paved streets, municipal buildings, mosques and a magnificent dockside, today offering stunning examples of period colonial architecture. With the end of the Raj and Partition in 1947, Karachi became Pakistan's capital. But it was replaced by Rawalpindi in 1958 and went into decline.

However, Karachi has reinvented itself in the 21st century as the commercial and technological hub of Pakistan, with its share of multi-millionaires and a

Ride a camel on the beach at Clifton.

burgeoning arts scene with the National Academy of Performing Arts, an annual music festival and the Kara Film Festival. But still there couldn't be a better place for enquiring families to see and appreciate the stark contrast between rich and poor that characterizes the developing Third World.

When the kids are fed up with shopping in Saddar, or the Empress Market, or the innumerable bazaars that line the streets, and everyone has admired the Quaid-e Azam Mausoleum and the largest single-domed mosque in the world (Masjid-e Tooba), and had their fill of colonial architecture...well, within minutes it's possible to ride a camel on the beach at Clifton, admire the world's second largest fountain at Seaview, enjoy a meal in one of the hip restaurants at Boat Basin, or just chill out on scarily high cliff tops above the sparkling Arabian Sea.

This is a multi-cultural city with unique character – a mixture of Western, South Asian and Middle Eastern influences give it an extraordinarily vibrant ambience. It is known locally as 'City of Lights' because of its liveliness. Its very vastness is a thrill in itself, and Karachi makes a wonderful tourist destination.

The tomb of Mohammed Ali Jinnah

FOLLOWING PAGES: The hustle and bustle of the Empress Market

Lahore

This one-time capital of the Mughal and later Sikh Empire is a city steeped in culture, learning and the arts. Lahore was renowned as a cultural centre by the 12th century, but really came to prominence in the 16th, when it became the quintessential Mughal city. When the British gained control in 1849, they restored much that had been damaged during Sikh rule and added some fine colonial gothic architecture, including the High Court and University buildings. It all makes for a fascinating – and educational – holiday destination.

Some of the finest surviving Mughal architecture in the world is here, including the World Heritage Site of Lahore Fort, a masterpiece containing mosques and palaces in marbles and mosaics. The Shalimar Gardens is a classic example of a Mughal terraced garden with channels, waterfalls and lodges in which to sit and admire the view. In the middle of Iqbal Park stands the national monument of Pakistan, Minar-e Pakistan – a 60-m (197-ft) tall minaret built on the spot where the Muslim League passed the Lahore Resolution demanding a homeland for the Muslims of India in 1940. Nearby is the magnificent 17th-century Badshahi Mosque, a striking building of red stone and white marble, one of the largest mosques in the Indian sub-continent. Much of the old city wall remains intact and the narrow lanes of the bazaars of the inner

The Lahore Fort – a masterpiece of Mughal architecture

city are a lively scrum of rickshaws, donkey carts and street hawkers. Anarkali is one of the oldest markets in South Asia, and Ichhra Bazaar is in a district of beautiful old *havelis* (historical houses).

Lahore lives up to its sobriquets of 'Garden of the Mughals' and the 'Heart of Pakistan'. It is one of the most beautiful, atmospheric, and cultured cities of South Asia as well as being a shoppers' paradise. No discerning visitor will ever be disappointed.

FOLLOWING PAGES: Sunset at the beautiful Badshahi Mosque

Chennai

Chennai, on the Coromandel Coast of the Bay of Bengal, is the capital of the Indian state of Tamil Nadu. It is the country's fourth-largest city and is renowned as a centre of south Indian music and dance, as well as for its architecture, cultural heritage, and wonderful sandy beaches. With lots to see and do, it makes a very rewarding destination for a different family holiday.

Kapaleeshwar – a fantastic example of Tamil architecture with intricate carvings

The city's origins go back to the 17th century. In 1639 the British East India Company struck a deal with the local nayak (ruler) to build a warehouse. In 1640 they constructed Fort St George, one of the first British bastions in India, which became the hub around which the city (called Madras until 1996) grew. Gradually they gained control of the region, although not before there was some serious wrangling with the French and much wheeling and dealing with local rulers. During the Raj, the city expanded to become a major commercial centre. All very exotic and exciting!

Chennai has a fascinating range of buildings. Much of the city retains a colonial feel, with long avenues of tall trees and fine Indo-Saracenic architecture (a style of building mixing Mughal with gothic).There is also the Portuguese 16th-century San Thome Basilica and the Kapaleeshwar Temple – a fantastic example of Dravidian (Tamil) architecture with intricate carvings. In the sprawling estate garden of the World Headquarters of the Theosophical Society (established here in 1886) there are shrines to all the major world faiths.

Chennai is a historic south Indian city with a leisurely pace of life and an entirely different, less frenetic atmosphere than the cities of the north. It is the base for the Tamil movie industry (dubbed Kollywood) which churns out 300 films a year, and the centre for Bharatanatyam classical dance.

WHEN TO GO:
Chennai is said to have three seasons – hot, hotter, and hottest. As good a time as any is Pongal (harvest festival), celebrated in January and lasting for five days.

TOP FAMILY ATTRACTIONS:
Guindy National Park – the only national park within a city (forests, lakes and streams to explore); Chennai Museum, a fabulous building stuffed with chaotic but riveting collections; Tamilnadu Science & Technology Centre with eight enlightening-for-kids galleries (also encompasses Birla Planetarium); Queens Land amusement park (off the Bangalore trunk road), featuring the heart-stopping Free Fall Tower (not for young children); Crocodile Bank, 40 km (25 mi) to the south of Chennai, for coastal dune forest that provides a haven for native wildlife, a nesting beach for sea turtles – and the biggest crocodile sanctuary in India.

YOU SHOULD KNOW:
The Chettinad regional cuisine of Tamil Nadu is famous throughout India and features hot and spicy meals that provide a delectable variety of mutton, chicken and fish dishes. But do be aware that 'hot' means HOT!

Delhi

The capital city of the world's largest democracy is also one of its oldest. There is evidence of human habitation from at least 2000 BC, and Delhi has not only seen empires rise and fall but has also been the capital of several of them.

Delhi is two separate cities. The city of the Mughals is Old Delhi while New Delhi was built to a grand design by the British architect Lutyens. Two broad central boulevards bisect each other. The Rajpath runs from the magnificent presidential palace, Rashtrapati Bhavan to India Gate, a spectacular arch commemorating the Indian soldiers who died fighting British wars. The Janpath leads to the main shopping district, Connaught Place, a series of elegant colonnaded terraces modelled on the Royal Crescent in Bath. It all seems splendidly familiar, including road congestion typical of all modern cities.

Old Delhi is another world. Chandni Chowk, the main thoroughfare, leads into a web of mysterious dark lanes and teeming bazaars, a maelstrom of traffic and people,

School transport in the Muslim district

The Red Fort

pariah dogs and flies and everywhere the smell of dust and incense, spices and sewage. After weaving your way through the street hawkers, mendicants, naked vagrants, wandering cows, bullock carts, snake charmers, cycle rickshaws, bedraggled women and children, the Red Fort is a soothing haven from sensory overload – a magnificent 17th-century Mughal seat of power with walls 2 km (1.25 mi) long, acres of garden and Chatta Chowk covered bazaar. Nearby is Jama Masjid – India's largest mosque with two 40-m (130-ft) minarets. The 13th-century Qutab Minar is even taller at 72.5 m (238 ft).

Delhi is a complex, challenging place – infuriating, fascinating, baffling, loathsome and wonderful in equal measure. It has to be seen to be believed and will be a real eye-opener for any family bold enough to dive in to the seething city with its colourful street life.

FOLLOWING PAGES: A boating lake next to India Gate

Bara Imam, a long corridor of rooms, at Chowmahalla Palace

Hyderabad

This cosmopolitan city is the capital of Andhra Pradesh state. It is renowned for its colourful history and superb architecture as well as its unique quality of life. Hyderabad is dotted with mosques, forts, palaces, tombs and temples, and on every street corner there are *irani chai* (tea) houses, where people sit for hours watching the world go by.

A Muslim ruler, Muhammad Quli Qutb Shah, founded Hyderabad on the southern side of the River Musi in 1586. He employed Persian architects to build him a city that would be a re-creation of Paradise. The central monument is the Charminar, a triumphal arch that Muhammad Quli had built in honour of his adored Hindu wife. It is a subtle mix of Islamic and South Indian architecture that embodies the culture of the city and stands as its icon. Nearby is the Makkah Masjid – the second-largest mosque in India, which took 78 years to build. The huge pink granite colonnades are each carved from a single block of stone. On a hilltop overlooking the city is the beautiful Birla Mandir – a marble Hindu temple dedicated to Laxmi (the goddess of prosperity) and Narayana (the preserver). The temple was inaugurated

WHEN TO GO:
November to February
TOP FAMILY ATTRACTIONS:
The sound and light show at Golconda Fort – one of the most magnificent fortress complexes in India, with a 10-km (6-mi) long outer wall and 87 bastions, 11 km (7 mi) away; Chowmahalla Palace – seat of the Nizam, with a beautiful garden; Saalar Jung Museum with its huge collection of assorted artefacts; Hyderabad Zoo (endangered animals a speciality, including tigers); Kasu Brahmananda Reddy (KBR) National Park at forested Jubilee Hill, providing a refuge for birds, reptiles and mammals (including jungle cats and mongoose); Ramoji Film City (RFC), one of the world's largest film studio complexes (tours and other entertainments); a trip out of town to Ocean Park, an amusement park at the Gandipet (Osman Sagar Lake) that caters for the whole family.

by Mahatma Gandhi on the condition that people of all castes will be allowed to enter.

A new dynasty was started by Asaf Jah in 1724. He entitled himself 'Nizam' (hereditary governor) and the city expanded to become capital of the largest princely state in India. To the south of the city is the 19th-century Italianate Falaknuma Palace, a stunning memorial to the Nizams' wealth. Their princely era finally ended in 1948 when Hyderabad was incorporated into the rest of India. Sometimes known as 'Cyberabad' for its thriving information technology industry, Hyderabad today is one of the most developed and also most interesting cities in India. It is a 21st-century city with its own unique heritage – a fascinating fusion of Islamic and ancient Southern Indian cultures. Seeing is believing!

YOU SHOULD KNOW:
The stunning 105-carat Koh-i-Noor Diamond ('Mountain of Light') came from diamond mines around Hyderabad that made the city rich. Hyderabad is also known as the 'city of pearls' and the famous pearl market in Patthargatti has every conceivable variety.

The Charminar embodies the culture of the city.

Udaipur

WHEN TO GO:
Mid September to early April
TOP FAMILY ATTRACTIONS:
Numerous palaces, including
those that featured in the
James Bond film *Octopussy*
(the Lake Palace and the
Monsoon Palace); Jagdish
Mandir, the largest temple in
Udaipur, with music and
chanting throughout the day;
Bagore-ki Haveli, a lovely 18th-
century residence on the
waterfront where you can see
displays of Rajasthani dancing
and music; Bharatiya Lok Kala
Mandal, an excellent folk art
museum; boat trips on the
most beautiful lakes in
Rajasthan – Pichola, Fateh
Sagar, Udai Sagar and Swaroop
Sagar; Gulab Bagh; a
wonderful rose garden laid out
by Maharaja Sajjan Singh
(within the garden is a zoo
with tigers and leopards, plus
a mini train).
YOU SHOULD KNOW:
Udaipur was the birthplace of
Bagheera the black panther, in
Rudyard Kipling's *The Jungle
Book*. Udaipur has been
ranked seventh-top city in the
world in a poll to decide top
international holiday
destinations.

If the family can visit but one Indian city, make it Udaipur. Rajasthan is renowned for its beautiful cities but this, the 'City of Lakes', is the most romantic of them all – a gleaming fantasy of 17th- and 18th-century palaces, temples, gardens, *havelis* (courtyard houses), bazaars and museums in a wonderful waterside setting.

According to legend the Rajput Maharana of Mewar, Udai Singh, was out hunting one day when he met a holy man who told him it was a favourable spot. So in 1559 he decided to build a palace here and in 1568 made Udaipur the capital of his kingdom.

A boat ride on Lake Pichola in the setting sun is enough to quicken the senses of even the most jaded travellers. There are two islands, on which stand magical gleaming white palaces – the Jag Niwas and the Jag Mandir. The lake is enclosed by hills, and the City Palace runs along the eastern bank. This magnificent building is one of the largest marble palaces in the world – a maze of courtyards, terraces, hanging gardens, cupolas and luxurious apartments.

To the north, the man-made Fateh Sagar lake has

a beautiful island housing the Nehru Garden, a huge
fountain and the Udaipur Solar Observatory. Perched
on the hillside overlooking the city is the Monsoon
Palace, the royal summer residence. And from the
Sajjan Niwas garden a short climb leads up to the
ridge of the old city wall, from where you can gaze
down over the plains. In the old city, curlicued stucco
work and colourful painting round the doorways of
the whitewashed *havelis* is straight out of a picture
book. Cows and elephants wander around the narrow
cobblestoned lanes of the bazaars where artisans ply
their trade. Udaipur really is a fairytale city, 'like no
other place on earth'.

*ABOVE AND FOLLOWING
PAGES: The Lake Palace*

Jaipur

Jaipur is one of the most important heritage cities in India and a major tourist attraction – a destination offering visitors of all ages a rewarding experience. This is the capital of Rajasthan, the ancient desert state of the Rajputs – a Hindu caste of warriors greatly respected and feared by both Mughals and the British. Jaipur is called the 'Pink City' after its ornately decorated stucco buildings, painted to replicate the sandstone of Mughal architecture.

The founder of Jaipur was a far-sighted astronomer king, Maharajah Sawai Jai Singh. Realizing that there would soon be a water shortage due to a growing population, he relocated his base in 1727. He designed his new city according to the principles of Shilpa-Shastra, an ancient Hindu architectural theory based on auspicious geometric and astrological lines. The old walled city is therefore laid out as a mandala in nine parts, one for each astrological sign, with broad streets and gardens.

The Chokri Sarhad is a huge palace complex, a striking blend of Mughal and Rajput design. The Maharajah's family still live in the Chandra Mahal. Opposite is the Jantar Mantar observatory and, abutting the palace wall, the Hawa Mahal (Palace of the Winds) – an archetypal example of Rajput architecture built for the royal women to see into the street without being seen themselves.

There are three stupendous forts on the edge of the city – the Amer, Jaigarh and Nahargarh – each in its own way attesting to the greatness of Rajput culture. The maharajahs of Jaipur were benevolent rulers, tolerant of other religions. Jainism flourished here and Jaipur is still one of the most important Jain centres in India.

Jaipur is heaven for shopping. Jauhari Bazaar and Badi Chaupar are full of traditional Rajput ornaments, paintings, block-printed textiles, carved wood, leather, precious and semi-precious stones, pottery – and the famous Jaipur quilts.

WHEN TO GO:
March, for Holi (the festival of colours) and the Elephant Festival. The truly steamy must-avoid months are June, July and August.

DON'T MISS:
Jal Mahal – a palace sitting in the middle of a lake filled with water hyacinths; the Jantar Mantar, an extraordinary collection of 18th-century architectural astronomical instruments; the Alice Garg National Seashells Museum, the only one of its kind in India; Ram Niwas Garden with the Albert Hall museum (holding a sumptuous collection showcasing the art of Jaipur) plus picnic areas, cafés, bird park, zoo, theatre, gymnasium and art gallery; the famous Amber Fort just outside town (and the adjoining Kanak Vrindavan garden and temple of Govind Deo Ji); a trip out to Chokhi Dhani – a funfair 18 km (11 mi) from the city centre where you can watch folk dancing, listen to traditional music, have elephant and camel rides and eat your fill.

YOU SHOULD KNOW:
This is a city that relies heavily on the tourist trade. If you want to photograph snake charmers, camel drivers, holy men or any other colourful character you are expected to pay, and it would be churlish not to. The only free photographic co-stars are members of the city's monkey colony, and even they are adroit at extracting treats.

LEFT: *The best way to approach the Amber Fort – by elephant!*

FOLLOWING PAGES: *A prettily decorated elephant walks past the Palace of the Winds (Hawa Mahal).*

Beijing

WHEN TO GO:
Any time, but September and October (the 'Golden Autumn') are best.
DON'T MISS:
The Forbidden City; an accessible section of the Great Wall of China at Badaling Pass some 55 km (34 mi) from the city – a great place to view one of the world's most awesome sights (magnificent views from the cable car that takes you to the top of the wall, or walk it if the family's feeling energetic); Beijing Zoo, the largest in China and (needless to say) one with a resident population of Giant Pandas (also the adjacent Beijing Aquarium); Taipingyang Underwater World with long transparent tunnel (automatic walkway); Happy Valley amusement park, boasting Asia's top six rides.
YOU SHOULD KNOW:
The Beijing Subway is a good way to get around the city quickly and is helpfully marked in English to assist travellers. This flat city is also made for bicycle exploration (by anyone brave enough to take on the mad traffic, which also makes crossing the road on foot a hazardous gamble). English is not widely spoken and it's helpful to get your hotel to make a list of places you want to visit using Chinese and Western characters, to show when asking directions or briefing a taxi driver.

The capital of the People's Republic of China, Beijing has been inhabited for well over 3,000 years and has history, tradition and architecture aplenty. After the years of the cultural revolution, economic activity in China is increasing hand over fist and nowhere more so than in Beijing. It's a must-visit powerhouse.

The main tourist jaw-dropper is the Imperial Palaces of the Forbidden City (now known as the Palace Museum) – the private Inner Court and the administrative areas of the Outer Court. Its entrance, the Tiananmen Gate – the Gate of Heavenly Peace – is the epitome of imperial architecture. It is a UNESCO World Heritage Site, as is the Summer Palace, a vast royal park whose landscape, lakes and buildings are designed to ensure that the viewer gets the most out of every viewpoint. There are more than 3,000 structures within the park. The third part of the trio of extensive Imperial sites is the Temple of Heaven, a huge temple complex with breath-taking buildings, while the Ming Dynasty Tombs are not only beautiful but important because of what they reveal about early medieval beliefs. There are more than 20 other important

TOP RIGHT AND RIGHT:
The Forbidden City is classified as a World Heritage Site by UNESCO.

The view over Hong Kong from the Peak tram.

Hong Kong

Hong Kong is part of Communist China yet distinct from Communist China – just one of a mass of contradictions that make this a most beguiling place for a family visit. It's an ultra-modern city where traditional values of hospitality are held dear, English pubs sit next to dim sum restaurants and double-decker trams pass hawkers selling chicken feet. This fusion of East and West is the legacy of a century and more of British

rule before the colony was returned to China in 1997.

The main entertainment and commercial areas are in the north of Hong Kong Island, while the east is residential and the south is green with pretty bays. Kowloon Peninsula is built up, while the New Territories and the Outlying Islands are more peaceful. Less well known are the beaches of Repulse Bay and the Outlying Islands and the hiking trails of the New Territories. The view from Victoria Peak across the city's soaring skyline is stunning. Ocean Park is beautiful. Shopping and nightlife in upmarket areas such as Central and Causeway Bay are among the best in the world. Mong Kok is the site of amazing Chinese markets, where vendors sell food, medicines, clothing and fabrics, knick-knacks and just about anything else you could ever want or need. The food in Hong Kong is first class, from international restaurants serving every type of food you can imagine to tasty street food sold on every corner.

Famed for its frenetic 24-hour lifestyle, shopping, street vendors and food stalls, bright lights, skyscrapers and a beautiful harbour, Hong Kong is one of the world's premier holiday destinations. It's a place visitors fall in love with and immediately start to think about a return visit.

WHEN TO GO:
Autumn or spring (can be very hot between June and September inclusive, and chilly in winter)

TOP FAMILY ATTRACTIONS:
Two trips across the harbour on the famous Star Ferry – one by day and one by night; riding the amazing Peak tram to the summit of Victoria Peak for a ride (and panoramic view) to remember for a long time; the Hong Kong Science Museum (over 500 exhibits, mostly hands on, including the amazing Energy Machine); the Space Museum, arranged around a planetarium); Global Geopark of China in the New Territories for eerily beautiful landforms and a glimpse of Hong Kong's surprisingly remote and beautiful 'back country'; Ocean Park, an oceanarium, marine mammal and animal park plus amusement park; Hong Kong Disneyland (if there's any time left after seeing everything else!).

YOU SHOULD KNOW:
Many shops shut for days during the Chinese New Year (check dates as they change from year to year), though some stay open and visitors can enjoy events such as lion dances, fireworks and parades.
An Octopus card provides instant electronic access to Hong Kong's public transport system. English is Hong Kong's official second language.

FOLLOWING PAGES:.
The Star Ferry and
city skyline from
Kowloon side

Macao

A former Portuguese colony that has been back in Chinese hands since 1999, Macao's culture is an amalgam of the two influences. The Historic Centre of Macao World Heritage Site includes 28 monuments and eight public squares, partly explained by the fact that the Portuguese were here from the mid-16th century. Their buildings dominate parts of the old town, epitomized in the main square, Largo do Senado. To the north are the ruins of St Paul's Cathedral, above it stands the Monte Fort. Between the square and the Cathedral is a splendid little church called St Dominic's.

The A-Ma Temple is one of the most important in the city, built in the mid-15th century and dedicated to the goddess Matsu. Her festival is in April. Other festivals include the Feast of the Drunken Dragon and the Feast of Bathing of Lord Buddha in May, the Dragon Boat festival in June and the Hungry Ghosts Festival in late August or early September.

The Macao Tower provides views across the city from the revolving restaurant at the top as well as some of the best food in the city, which is saying a great deal. The food here is varied – Cantonese cuisine and ingredients mingle with Portuguese, Brazilian,

Goan and Angolan dishes. This is fusion food at its best! Family visitors need not be put off by the fact that most people come to Macao for the gambling. The Venetian, a huge and glitzy casino resort on the Cotai strip modelled on its sister resort in Las Vegas, is drawing more gamblers to the island than ever before. But they head for the bright, pocket-emptying lights of the gaming establishments, leaving the rest of this delightful former colonial enclave to visitors who can simply enjoy it for its own sake.

The façade of St Paul's Cathedral is Macao's most famous site.

Shanghai

WHEN TO GO:
Spring, summer or autumn, because air pollution can be a real problem in the painfully hot summer months of July and August.

TOP FAMILY ATTRACTIONS:
Shopping on the Nanjing Road, with a bonus for the kids – a miniature train transports foot-weary shoppers from one end to the other; the world-renowned Shanghai Museum; Shanghai Ocean Aquarium, boasting the world's longest underwater transparent tunnel and a giant goldfish named after Bruce Lee; Dino Beach Water Park ('Tropical Storm' in Chinese) – the beach is fake but the awesome wave machine isn't; Jinjiang Action Park, an amusement park with more than 30 rides and attractions; Circus World – an indoor circus that puts on spectacular shows, notably acrobatics.

YOU SHOULD KNOW:
The number of road fatalities in Shanghai is scarily high and the general standard of driving is somewhere between reckless and lethal via hair-raising. Take care when crossing roads and look out for motorbikes or scooters taking shortcuts across pavements. Steaming hot Shanghai dumplings are a must-taste culinary experience.

FOLLOWING PAGES:
The Bund offers great views over to the ever-changing skyline of Pudong.

RIGHT: Nanjing Road's miniature train

The largest industrial city in China, Shanghai sits on the estuary of the Yangtze River. It is a fascinating, frenetic city where the best of traditional and modern China combine seamlessly. The iconic modern skyline of Pudong, world-class shopping and food, the culture and traditional buildings are among the finest in the country. It's an ideal destination for adventurous families.

For sightseeing and shopping, the areas around People's Square and along the Huangpu River have much to offer. Nanjing Road and Huaihai Road are where the best fashion shops are to be found and the latter is also known for its antique shops, cafés and the charming French Concession area. Wander along The Bund to admire historical buildings and great views across the river to Pudong. For weary families wanting a break from the frantic pace of the city (and the constant soundtrack of car horns), the Yuyuan Garden offers welcome respite. This is a beautiful and tranquil enclave where bamboos, stone bridges, ponds with koi carp and rock gardens combine to create a serene atmosphere.

Among the old buildings in the city are the Longhua Pagoda, the Jade Buddha Temple and the Tomb of Lu Xun. Chongming Island, Zhujajiao Water Town and Qibao Ancient Town are also worth visiting. Cultural highlights include the Shanghai Museum and performances in the Shanghai Grand Theatre, both of which are amazing modern buildings.

But take the time to stray away from the usual tourist haunts, fashionable shops and the alluring glare of the neon lights. Wander down side streets to discover a world away from the polished, modernized China this schizophrenic country wants the world to see. Here you will gain real insight into Chinese culture and traditions as inhabitants go about their daily lives, seemingly oblivious to your presence.

Suzhou

WHEN TO GO:
Spring or autumn (July and August are much too hot).
TOP FAMILY ATTRACTIONS:
The classical gardens; Pan Gate Scenic Area for the 'three landmarks' (Ruiguang Pagoda, built in 247 BC, Wu Gate Bridge and Pan Gate); Huangcangyu Nature Reserve – a most attractive green enclave with forests, caves, springs, pools and temples; the Silk Museum, documenting the long tradition of local silk-making (but kids will only have eyes for the room full of live silk worms, eating mulberry leaves and spinning valuable cocoons); Suzhou Amusement Land for family fun (four stomach-churning roller coasters and other attractions).
YOU SHOULD KNOW:
Bikes can easily be rented and cycling is an interesting if hair-raising way of exploring Suzhou. A network of cycle paths run alongside most roads though these also serve as scooter rat-runs, pedestrian walk-ways and illegal parking places so it's advisable not to glance at passing sights without stopping first.

Perhaps now best known for traditional waterside architecture and beautiful gardens, Suzhou was the capital of the Wu kingdom for more than eight centuries and a centre of the silk industry. This major city is in southeast Jiangsu Province in Eastern China, adjacent to Shanghai Municipality. It is often referred to as the 'Venice of the East'.

Culturally aware (and/or green-fingered) families will be delighted to find a beautiful garden at almost every turn. To emphasize their importance, these outstanding gardens have been listed as a UNESCO World Heritage Site since 1997. Among the best are the Humble Administrator's Garden (Zhou Zheng Yuan), the Garden of the Master of the Nets (Wang Shi Yuan) and the Surging Wave Pavilion (Canglangting). The classic Mountain Villa with Embracing Beauty (Huanxiu Shanzhuang) is one of the most important water-and-rock gardens. There are smaller gardens dotted throughout the city and these are usually more peaceful places to relax. Typical examples of these small havens are the Wufeng Xianguan and Yi Yuan gardens.

The city also has many traditional buildings that should not be missed, including the Beisi, North and Yunyan pagodas, Cold Mountain Temple, Pan Gate and the Baodai Bridge. Historic Pingjiang Road and ancient Shantang Road are on the list of China's 'famous

historical and culture streets', each featuring elegant bridges, flowing waters and unique architecture.

But a visit can be about much more than wonderful old buildings and gardens. Suzhou is also renowned for its arts and crafts. The Kunqu form of Chinese opera originates here, and Suzhou Pingtan is a captivating local storytelling tradition that involves singing. Silk and embroidery are important, as is jade carving. For a taste of old China, with all its culture and traditions set in a beautiful landscape, this is a very good place to visit.

Suzhou's streets are lined with historic buildings.

The iconic Kobe Port Tower has an observation deck with great views.

Kobe

In 1868, after the prolonged isolation of the late Edo period, Kobe was one of the first cities in Japan to become open for trade with other countries. Since then the city has become Japan's fifth-largest, a cosmopolitan and welcoming place that makes for an interesting opportunity to explore Japanese culture during a stimulating family holiday.

The beautiful Ikuta Shrine is the most important

monument and might be described as the city's raison-d'être. According to literature, it was founded in the early third century as part of military rites and the forest behind it is dotted with markers commemorating battles. Other important shrines include Nagata-ku, which was established at the same time.

Nowadays Kobe is renowned as a centre of the fashion industry and its chief shopping areas are Motomachi and Sannomiya, which are also hubs of night life. Next to Motomachi lies the city's Chinatown – Nankinmachi – a thriving area with bustling street life. One of the most iconic structures in town is Kobe Port Tower, a strangely shaped metal structure (technically known as a hyperboloid). It's 108 m (over 350 ft) high, with an observation deck near the top which has great views out over the port. The outlook across the Akashi Strait from the Akashi-Kaikyo suspension bridge is also stunning, as is that from the Venus Bridge.

Kobe sits at the foot of the iconic Rokko mountain range with its popular walking, hiking and sightseeing areas, easily accessed from the city by cable car. It is home to Japan's first golf course (of many!). The mountains are noted for autumn colours and the famous hot springs of the Arima onsen, which lie on the other side of the range, definitely merit a family excursion.

WHEN TO GO:
Any time of year

TOP FAMILY ATTRACTIONS:
A harbour boat cruise; the Maritime Museum in a stunning modern building with a billowing roofline of metal sails, containing wonderfully detailed ship models (also includes a Kawasaki hi-tech display with interactive models featuring company products from motorcycles to the Shinkansen bullet train); Harborland – a regenerated dockland area with hotels, shops and amusements including a ferris wheel; the Shin-Kobe Ropeway (cablecar) with one of Kobe's best scenic views, running up to the Nunobiki herb park; Kobe Science Museum – good interactive exhibits but limited English support (closed on Wednesdays); Oji Zoo – animals plus mini amusement park with rides for youngsters; Toba Aquarium, specializing in unusual sea creatures such as dugong (sea cows).

YOU SHOULD KNOW:
In 1995 the devastating Kobe (Great Hanshin) earthquake killed 6,433 people, who are commemorated in Meriken Park near the harbour. The city holds a remembrance day celebrating its subsequent recovery every December.

Osaka

Jurassic Park: The Ride at Universal Studios

Osaka is not only a vibrant modern city, but also the site of one of the most ancient settlements in Japan, having been important as a sea and river port on and off for many centuries. Today, Osaka is one of Japan's major commercial and shipping hubs and is internationally famous for gourmet food and power shopping in the Minimi's Namba, Dotonbori, Amerikamura and Shinsaibashi areas, as well as Den Den Town (for electricals) and the longest shopping arcade in Japan, Tenjinbashi-suji.

The city has a wealth of temples and shrines, including Shitenno-ji, reputed to be the first Buddhist temple in Japan, and Sumiyoshi Taisha, one of the earliest Shinto shrines, thought to date back to the early third century. Osaka's long history and culture are celebrated in many museums and galleries, including the Osaka Museum of History; the Museum of Oriental Ceramics; Osaka Prefectural Museum of Kamigata Comedy & Performing Arts and the Osaka Municipal Museum of Art. There are also science, natural history and children's museums. The National Museum of Art is underground and its collections concentrate on modern art. The city is also known for its traditional kabuki and *bunraku* (puppet) theatres.

Other attractions include Shin-Umeda City, with its

WHEN TO GO:
Any time of year
TOP FAMILY ATTRACTIONS:
Panoramic views from Shin-Umeda City or the Tsutenkaku Tower; the Science Museum – theme 'The Universe and Energy', numerous exciting interactive exhibits plus planetarium and Omnimax theatre for space-hoppers; Tennŷji Zoo, cleverly arranged so that carnivorous animals and herbivores seem to be sharing the same patch of savannah; Osaka Aquarium Kaiyukan, the second largest in the world; Universal Studios Japan, a theme park based on the Universal Orlando Resort in Florida, with film-themed rides (such as Jurassic Park: The Ride).

floating garden observatory 170 m (560 ft) above ground, an underground shopping centre and Zen garden. Osaka Castle Garden is a favourite place for both locals and tourists, especially when the cherry trees are in blossom, although the castle itself is a reproduction. Other open spaces include Nakanoshima Park, Sumiyoshi Park and Tennoji Park, designed by one of the country's best gardeners, Jihei Ogawa. In addition to all the city's cultural attractions, there's plenty of 21st-century-style entertainment on offer for younger family members.

YOU SHOULD KNOW:
Fugu restaurants are a major aspect of culinary life in Osaka – *fugu* is the Japanese for 'pufferfish' but indulging in this renowned Japanese delicacy is not for the faint-hearted. If prepared incorrectly it can be lethal!

Cherry blossom at Osaka Castle

Tokyo

WHEN TO GO:
Any time of year (but those cherry trees beloved by the Japanese blossom in March and April).

TOP FAMILY ATTRACTIONS:
Everyone should see it, so a trip out of town to iconic Mount Fuji should be high on every family's worth-visiting list; the Eiffel-Tower style Tokyo Tower, Japan's second-highest structure at 332.5 m (1,091 ft) for fabulous views from the observation deck; National Museum of Nature and Science for interactive scientific experiences and natural history displays; Mount Takao – offering a relaxing break from the hustle and bustle of city streets with its temple, nature walks, waterfalls and monkey park (walk up the mountain, take the cable car or ride the exciting chair lift); Ueno Park with its museums, small amusement park and other attractions – notably the zoo; Epson Aqua Stadium at the Prince Hotel, an aquarium with dolphin, seal and penguin shows plus hundreds of species of fish (also a carousel ride); Tokyo Disneyland for all the fun of the Magic Kingdom.

YOU SHOULD KNOW:
Tokyo has an extensive and efficient mass transit system but it's potentially confusing to visitors because several distinct railway systems operate within the city – JR East network, two subway networks plus private lines – and different route maps show different systems. Whichever one(s) you use, avoid rush-hour travel if you suffer from a sardine-tin phobia.

Tokyo is one of the busiest cities on the planet and the pace of life never slows, energizing visitors and making for an exciting family holiday. From sightseeing outside the Imperial Palace to shopping in the 'Little Hong Kong' complex in Odaiba everything happens at breakneck pace. A thriving town called Edo since the early 17th century, it became the new capital of Japan when Emperor Meiji moved the imperial court here in 1869.

As well as some of the best shopping in the world in places such as Ginza, Shibuya, Ikebukero and Shinjuku, Tokyo is home to a rich variety of cultural attractions. In Ueno Park, the Tokyo National Museum has 20 galleries filled with stunning artefacts from 1,500 years of Japanese history. The National Museum of Western Art nearby has a large collection of Impressionist works, and other institutions include the Municipal Art Gallery, National History Museum, National Science Museum and the Gallery of Far Eastern Art.

The city is also home to the Shinjuku Gyoen National Garden, which has both Japanese and European style gardens, and a tea-house where visitors can take part in the traditional tea ceremony. The area is also a very popular centre for entertaining street

life, as is the Roppongi quarter. Ginza is home to the Kabuki-za Theatre.

In Asakusa, you will find the Sensoji Temple, the Five-storied Pagoda and Nakamise, a traditional shopping arcade, as well as the Hanayashiki Amusement Park. Harajuku is where the young hang out, while Azabu-Juban is upmarket and Akihabara is the place to buy electronics. But whatever the family looks for in a city, Tokyo has it in spades, from beautiful gardens to theme parks, from fine art galleries to the biggest fish markets in the world, from bullet trains to theme parks.

FOLLOWING PAGES:
Fuji-Hakone-Izu
National Park

Sensoji Temple

Luang Prabang

WHEN TO GO:
Any time of year
TOP FAMILY ATTRACTIONS:
A Mekong River sightseeing
cruise, which could take in Pak
Ou Caves (about two hours
upstream from Luang Prabang)
featuring hundreds of Buddha
statues on wall shelves; Kuang
Si Falls, a three-tier cascade
some 30 km (18 mi) south of
town with walkways, bridges
and blue pools for wild
swimming (also visit the
adjacent bear sanctuary);
Elephant Village in a lush
valley on the banks of the
Nam Khan River 15 km (10 mi)
south-east of Luang Prabang
in the ancient village of
Xieng Lom (elephant rides,
jungle hiking).

*An elephant trek
through the jungle near
Luang Prabang*

The Laoatian city of Luang Prabang is located where
the mighty Mekong and Khan rivers meet, complete
with atmospheric backdrop of misty hills. This
fascinating city was the royal capital from the 14th
century until the Lao monarchy was overthrown by
Communists in 1975. A UNESCO World Heritage Site as
the best-preserved city in south-east Asia, it is also one
of the most beautiful, amply justifying a long-haul
family visit.

Luang Prabang is celebrated for temples and
monasteries. Distinctive golden temple roofs
dominate the old city, prayer flags flutter in the breeze
and evocative gongs echo around the town. A major
attraction is the Royal Palace (Haw Kham), built near
the river in 1904 for King Sisavang Vong so that official
visitors could disembark from their boats directly below
the palace. Crown Prince Savang Vatthana and his
family were the last to occupy the palace before the
monarchy was overthrown and the Royal Family
summarily dispatched to re-education camps. The
palace is now a museum, and should be visited.

A colourful market in Luang Prabang

Xiang Thong is the main street of the city, lined with traditional Lao wooden houses mixed with European architecture, reminders of the French Colonial era. Temples decorated with mosaics and murals of the Buddha sit beside 19th-century shuttered windows and decorative balconies. Strolling around this atmospheric city through pretty streets shaded with palms and flowering trees is a peaceful and uplifting experience. If the family tires of temples and palaces, climb Phou Si Hill to watch the sunset or enjoy leisurely refreshments beside the river. Shop in the bustling markets or visit one of the many monasteries – Wat Xiang Thong is the oldest in the city and one of the most beautiful, a perfect place to soak up Luang Prabang's serene and spiritual atmosphere. Don't expect glitzy tourist attractions, because simply being here is enough.

YOU SHOULD KNOW:
If visiting from Thailand it's possible to take a leisurely slow boat down the mighty Mekong River to Luang Prabang from Huay Xai on the border (two days with an overnight stop in Pakbeng), which is a great way to get an authentic flavour of Laos. Those in a hurry can take a bone-shaking speedboat ride and make the same journey in just six exhilarating hours.

Hoh Chi Minh City

TOP FAMILY ATTRACTIONS:
French-built Notre Dame Catholic Cathedral in the city centre; the General Library, if only to see one of the finest buildings in Vietnam; Ben Thanh Market for an authentic slice of Vietnamese city life; Reunification Palace – formerly South Vietnam's Presidential Palace, left 'as was', complete with a replica of the original tank that crashed through the gates, symbolically ending the Vietnam War; the emotive War Remnants Museum (once provocatively called 'The Exhibition of American War Crimes'), to provide youngsters with some understanding of the horror of war; Dam Sen Water Park with its spectacular water slides; one of the oldest zoos in the world, Saigon Zoo and Botanical Garden, for rare orchids, ornamental plants, and an impressive collection of mammals, reptiles and birds; a choice of Vietnamese-style amusement parks, Dam Sen, Suoi Tien and Dai Nam.

YOU SHOULD KNOW:
Be aware if visiting attractions with animals that Vietnamese welfare standards are towards the non-existent end of the spectrum. Taking taxis in HCMC can be a lottery – there are reputable taxi firms but also scam artists who paint their cabs to look like the real thing and charge outrageous fares, or even drive off with luggage still aboard as soon as they're paid.

HCMC's People's Committee Building, (Hotel de Ville)

The largest city in Vietnam is located on the banks of the Saigon River near the delta of the Mekong River. Until 1976 this was Saigon – under-siege capital of South Vietnam. Following its conquest by the Vietnam People's Army it became Hoh Chi Minh City, renamed in honour of North Vietnam's revolutionary leader, who died in 1969.

Everyone abbreviates the name to HCMC or continues to use Saigon. This great city is the fast-beating heart of Vietnam and offers more than it's possible for visiting families to see and do in a month, although the effort can be a real pleasure. The place is dynamic and industrious, serving as the country's economic and cultural focus. Those who know say it is hardly changed from pre-Communist days, although there has been a great deal of modern development since 1975.

There are plenty of interesting old buildings, museums and galleries to be found in HCMC, as would be expected in a former French colonial capital, plus some striking modern architecture. But the real joy of this vibrant place is the city life of South East Asia as it really is. The traffic – largely consisting of overloaded motorbikes and scooters – is ferocious, with little respect for small details like pavements and pedestrians, although there are miraculously few accidents. There are endless bars, restaurants, markets, street vendors and the old-fashioned cafés famous for strong coffee brewed in the cup.

This is a city of contrasts, with traditional ways of doing things rubbing shoulders with modern developments and the increasingly international character of a 21st-century city. This juxtaposition of old and new is never more striking than at the Phung Son Tu Pagoda, a small and dusty oasis of peace surrounded by the high rises of modern Ho Chi Minh City.

187

Wat Chedi Sao

Lampang

A stop on the Bangkok to Chiang Mai railway line,
Lampang attracts more Thai tourists than foreigners
and as a result is charmingly low-key. Founded in the
seventh century beside the Wang River, Lampang was
always a success. By the late 1800s it had carved itself
an important place in the teak trade, inspiring a
British-owned company to bring in loggers from
Burma, then part of the Empire, to harvest the
surrounding teak forests. Wealthy Burmese teak and
opium merchants built gorgeous wooden houses and
sponsored new temples, which can still be seen.

The first thing to strike the visitor arriving in town

is the number of horse-drawn carriages, a delightful form of public transport. What better way could there be for the family to go sightseeing than to be clip-clopping along, a Thai in a cowboy hat in the driver's seat acknowledging his colleagues with cheery waves of his whip. Wat Phra Kaew Don Tao is an impressive Burmese style temple on the north side of the river where the Emerald Buddha, Thailand's talisman, resided from 1436 to 1468. Today the most sympathetic structure in the complex is a crumbling old brick temple, set between trees covered with Buddhist maxims.

Don't miss Many Pillars House. Built in 1896, this wonderful example of a wealthy Lanna-style home is full of enough Burmese and Thai antiques to make your mouth water. Walk through streets of lovely wooden shop-houses, wander along the river and stop for sunset refreshments or a meal at one of the old traditional bars at the water's edge. It's a delight to be in a city not particularly geared to foreigners (no amusement parks, just local colour and culture), where the iced coffee is good and scrumptious food can be eaten in the company of Thais rather than visiting Westerners.

Wat Prathat Lampang Luang – a magnificent temple complex

Manila

An important trading centre since the late 16th century and capital of the Philippines under Spanish rule, Manila is one of the world's most cosmopolitan cities. It will be a real eye-opener for visiting families, with much to see and lots to do. Originally inhabited by the Tagalogs, successive waves of migration and invasion took place from regional tribes, Spaniards in the 1570s, Chinese, all-conquering Americans in the

WHEN TO GO:
Any time of year, although December to February are the most pleasant months (the rainy season is from June to October).

TOP FAMILY ATTRACTIONS:
Baywalk riverside park – the city's main promenade and a great place to watch Manilan life go by (and also watch fabulous sunsets); Manila Zoo and wildlife sanctuary (slightly run down but worth a look, also tranquil botanical gardens); Manila Butterfly House; Manila Ocean Park, a large modern aquarium complex with the mandatory long underwater tunnel; Manila Amusement Park with assorted rides and attractions for all ages; Enchanted Kingdom theme park to the south of the city.

YOU SHOULD KNOW:
There is an abundance of street food on offer in Manila, but visitors should note that there is little or no regulation and hygiene standards will vary from vendor to vendor. That said, the variety on offer is very tempting and bold visitors can enjoy some wonderful culinary treats.

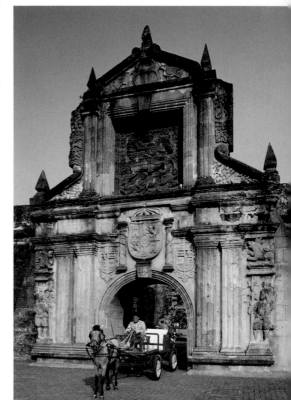

The main gate of Fort Santiago in the Intramuros Historical District

1890s and then the Japanese in the 1940s.

The historic city – Intramuros – is surrounded by walls erected by the Spanish and many of the city's highlights are contained within this area. Enjoy visiting old colonial buildings and churches, including Manila Cathedral, the San Agustin Church and Museum complex. The Bahay Tsinoy Museum is here, illuminating Chinese influence on the city. Other important museums include the Intramuros Light and Sound Museum, the Museo ng Maynila (Museum of Manila) and the Children's Museum (Museo Pambata). Pre-conquest culture can be explored in the Museum of the Parish of Our Lady of the Abandoned (Santa Ana).

Chinatown is a must for visitors, with bustling restaurants and shops, food markets and, paradoxically, one of the best Baroque cathedrals in the western hemisphere. In the Old Palace neighbourhood you will find not only Malacanang Palace itself (now a museum), but also the Church of San Sebastian, constructed entirely in steel, and some of the best-preserved colonial architecture in the city. Fans of Art Deco architecture should head to the campus of the Far Eastern University, a complex of 'modern' architecture with stunning murals and sculptures. Manila's cultural diversity is represented in its wide variety of religious sites, from synagogues to Spanish-style churches, Chinese and Hindu temples and mosques. It's all very appealing, and many visitors are drawn back again and again.

A Jeepney (painted Jeep), one of the local minibuses

Cable cars to Sentosa Island

Singapore

WHEN TO GO:
January to May (although the tropical climate means temperature, humidity and rainfall are consistently high).

TOP FAMILY ATTRACTIONS:
Esplanade Theatres on the Bay, alongside Marina Bay near the mouth of the Singapore River, for all the performing arts in a spectacular setting; a ride to the heavens on the Singapore Flyer, a giant observation wheel that rises to an awesome height of 165 m (541 ft); Jurong Bird Park with its many themed habitats and performing bird shows (also a unique monorail); Singapore Zoo, with over 300 species (many endangered) displayed in a naturalistic setting (also offers a wonderful night safari from the comfort of an open tram); Universal Studios Singapore on Sentosa resort

One of the few city-states in the world, Singapore is spread over 63 islands covering 705 sq km (272 sq mi) at the southern tip of the Malay Peninsula. In 1819, when still a sparsely populated fishing village, it was colonized by the British East India Company in order to exploit its geographical position as a tactical outpost along the wealth-generating Spice Route.

Occupied by the Japanese during World War II, Singapore subsequently reverted to British rule, later becoming part of the merger that established Malaysia in 1963. Two years later it became an independent republic. Since that time the state has seen a dramatic economic boom, helped by both foreign investment and government-led industrialization. This created a modern economy based on electronics and manufacturing. Singapore has a major foreign exchange trading centre and features in the world's 'Top Twenty' richest nations.

At first sight, visiting families may find Singapore's spotless streets lined with concrete-and-glass architecture strikingly modern and rather soulless. However, beneath the glitzy surface of Orchard Road's designer complexes lies a wealth of multi-cultural diversity. This undeniably Asian city unites Malay, Chinese, Indian, Arabic and European traditions, from ancestor worship to horse racing, to create a colourfully contrasting landscape of vibrant diffusion that makes for a visit to remember.

Wander the streets of Chinatown, Little India and Geylang Serai to get a feel for the city's segregated past. Visit the colourful Sri Mariamman Temple, admire orchids in 67 hectares (166 acres) of botanical gardens and indulge in some of the world's most delicious and diverse cuisine from the abundant hawker markets and food stalls. And, if the humidity gets too much, it's more than possible to recapture the colonial era whilst reclining with a leisurely cup of tea beneath one of Raffles Hotel's lazy fans.

island, the theme park where Hollywood comes to town; Marine Life Park (the world's largest) for dolphin interaction and much more, plus Maritime Museum (see the treasure ship!) and aquarium.

YOU SHOULD KNOW:
The nation's official first language is English. Singlish, the local colloquial dialect of English that has many Creole-like characteristics and also incorporates vocabulary and grammar from various Chinese dialects, Malay and Indian languages, is commonly spoken on the streets of Singapore. Dining and shopping are said to be the country's national pastimes.

Singapore's Monorail to Sentosa Resort Island

Ubud

WHEN TO GO:
Any time (but be aware that serious rain gear should be taken if visiting in January and February).

TOP FAMILY ATTRACTIONS:
Nightly dance and musical performances that bring Balinese culture to vibrant life; the Botanic Garden for ravines, groves, meadows, river, waterfalls and natural forest – plus orchid houses, themed gardens and Bali's first maze; Bali Bird and Reptile Park, set in landscaped gardens, offering a fine collection of around one thousand exotic birds from Indonesia, Africa and South America; Taro Elephant Safari Park, set in tropical parklands and forest to the northeast of the city – home to Sumatran elephants (feed them, ride them, watch their daily show, look round the elephant museum); a short trip out of town to the amazing Elephant Cave (Goa Gajah), one of Bali's most important historical sites, complete with entrance formed as a demonic face with fanged mouth.

YOU SHOULD KNOW:
This is the place to discover (and consume!) some of the best food in Indonesia. For family trips out of town hire a minivan or offroader (with driver) – a circular yellow 'E' on the windscreen certifies them as legitimate (don't forget to haggle about the price).

Located in Indonesia's central Bali, Ubud has changed from an artists' colony and backpackers' hideaway in a sleepy backwater to a sophisticated town that welcomes holidaymakers with fantastic museums, traditional mansions and stunning architecture, all set in a beautiful landscape. It is also Bali's centre for fine arts, crafts, dance and music. In the early part of the 20th century Westerners such as Walter Spies and Willem Hofker collected together the best Balinese artists in an informal training academy and thus established Ubud as an artistic centre. Their legacy lives on in the many museums here, including the Museum of Fine Arts, the Seniwati Gallery of Art by Women and the Museum Rudana, and in the thriving artistic tradition of the town and surrounding area.

Many of the villages around Ubud are home to specialist art and craft communities set among

Children at a local dance school

traditional rice terraces, ancient temples and idyllic landscapes. A particular feature of the area is the palaces *puris* – which housed the local princes. One of the best is the Puri Saren Agung, once the home of Tjokorde Gede Agung Sukawati, the last King of Ubud. His family still live here and host frequent dance performances. Other buildings and monuments include many beautiful temples such as the Pura Taman Saraswati. At Pejeng, just outside town, temples include the Goa Gaja, Pura Kebo Edan, Pura Pusering Jagat and Pura Agung Batan Bingin. The 14th-century reliefs of Yeh Pulu are among the best to be found in Asia.

The many artistic activities here give the city and surrounding area a unique character and when combined with the vibrant colours of the surrounding landscape, Ubud ticks all the boxes required for a memorable family holiday.

Three Hindu temples to Shiva, Brahma and Vishnu at Pura Taman Saraswati

AFRICA

Luxor

WHEN TO GO:
October to May
TOP FAMILY ATTRACTIONS:
First, foremost and all of them
most impressive – as much of
Luxor's amazing Ancient
Egyptian heritage as possible;
Luxor Museum for artefacts
galore; a hot-air balloon trip
over the Valley of the Kings
(expensive but a great
experience); a guided tour of
the ACE animal centre, caring
for Luxor's working and often
over-worked animals (and
others); the Karnak Sound and
Light Show, bringing the
dramatic early history of
Thebes to life.
YOU SHOULD KNOW:
Karnak was built over 1,300
years. At its peak it owned,
among other things, 422,000
cattle, 2,400 sq km (926 sq mi)
of fields, 65 villages, 83 ships
and 81,322 slaves and
workers. Hardly surprising –
pleasing the gods was big
business in Ancient Egypt, as
Luxor amply demonstrates to
this day. Take a torch – it's
dark in a lot of tombs and the
lights don't always work.

If the family wants to see Pharaonic Egypt in all its glory, a visit to Luxor is just the ticket. A city unlike any other on earth, the extraordinary quality, quantity and scale of its monuments along the Nile is impossible to appreciate without seeing them. Visitors have always come here, but despite today's tour buses and fleets of Nile cruisers it's still possible to be alone in front of a superb bas-relief carved over 3,000 years ago.

Known as Thebes, the city's glory days were between 1540-1069 BC, following the reunification of the country by Montuhotep II and relocation of his capital here. The Temple of Karnak, dedicated to the god Amun, is gigantic – its Hypostyle Hall, just one part of the complex, could easily hold Notre Dame Cathedral. In golden afternoon light the sight of 134 enormous columns soaring upwards, casting diagonal shadows, is astounding.

Luxor Temple, started by Amenhotep III and added to by many including Tutankhamun and Ramses II, overlooks the Nile. The avenue of Sphinxes, obelisks, papyrus columns, monumental gateways, huge statues and spectacular reliefs must be seen. Floodlit at night, it is magnificent. Crossing to the west bank, you'll suddenly come upon the Colossi of Memnon, all that remains of Amenhotep III's funerary temple, once as large as Karnak. The great necropolis in the Valley of the Kings contains 62 excavated tombs, the most beautifully decorated of which is probably that of Seti I. Hatshepsut's Temple and the Temple of Ramses III are both majestic sights.

Luxor town itself is full of hotels, restaurants and shops. Persistent hustlers suggest felucca trips, caleche tours, taxi hire and much more. Hire bicycles and set off early, resting up somewhere during the midday sun, and get going again later. By the evening, after a hearty meal, everyone will have just enough energy left to fall into bed.

FOLLOWING PAGES:
The Temple of Deir
El-Bahri on the West
Bank at Luxor

RIGHT: The head of
Ramses I, Luxor Temple

Sousse

Lying on the Gulf of Hammamet, Sousse is a lovely, lively place for the family to visit, combining the pleasures of a seaside resort with the exotic delights of a beautiful old medina surrounded by crenellated walls. Some two hours from Tunis, Sousse has a long history – Phoenicians, Romans, Byzantines and Arabs all settled here and left their mark.

By the ninth century this was already an important trading and military port town. The medina here, listed by UNESCO in 1988, is not huge but is certainly large enough to get lost in. Many of its twisting alleyways are covered by vaulted brickwork, and lovely tiles decorate the walls. Here you can spend hours haggling for carpets, leather ware, silver or pure woollen blankets and, if you're really smart, return home with a bargain. The Great Mosque is a simple, austere building, its sole decoration being the arches within. Although most mosques have a minaret this one has a cupola, added as recently as the 11th century.

The city's Archaeological Museum (second only to the Bardo Museum in Tunis) can be found in the 9th-century Khalef al Fata tower in the Kasbah, on the outskirts of the medina. It contains a collection of largely Roman mosaics, statues and tombs, including an amazing head of Medusa. The view from the tower is splendid. The Ribat, a smaller, square fort with tower, is within the medina – built in 820 by Islamic warrior monks to protect the population.

When the family tires of sightseeing and shopping head off to the long, sandy, northern beach with its string of modern hotels. Sousse is the holiday venue of choice for many Tunisians, and the beach nearest the centre of town is often crowded with friendly locals enjoying themselves in the sunshine.

The vibrant city of Sousse

Saint-Louis sits at the mouth of the Senegal River.

Saint-Louis

The old colonial city of Saint-Louis lies at the mouth of the Senegal River, a mere 10 km (6 mi) south of the border with Mauritania. Made up of three parts, the heart of Saint-Louis lies on a narrow island in the river. Separated from the Atlantic Ocean by a sand spit known as the Langue de Barbarie, also part of the city, it is connected by two bridges. The island is similarly joined to the mainland and the third part of the city, by the Faidherbe Bridge, constructed in 1897

on the orders of, and named after, Louis Faidherbe, the French colonial governor.

A fortified trading post was established on the then-uninhabited island of N'dar by French traders in 1659. The first permanent French settlement in Senegal, it was named after Louis XIV and was the centre of trade along the river. Slaves, beeswax, hides and ambergris were all exported from here and the city rapidly became a major economic player. A Franco-African Creole community of merchants, the Métis, sprang up, producing a vibrant and distinctive urban culture. During the late 1800s Louis Faidherbe was responsible for modernizing and developing Saint-Louis, but the city declined as Dakar gained in importance. Today, Saint-Louis is still a trading centre, but tourism has become more important to its economy. New restaurants and hotels are opening and it makes an interesting destination for an out-of-the ordinary family holiday.

Most of the colonial architecture is on the island and consists of two-storey buildings, the ground floors often shops, with red-tiled roofs, high wooden ceilings, wooden shutters and balconies with wrought iron balustrades. More imposing buildings include the old governor's palace. Saint-Louis is close to excellent national parks and long sandy beaches. It is renowned for its music festivals and the annual, lantern-lit procession that takes place in December.

WHEN TO GO:
November to May (the dry season).

TOP FAMILY ATTRACTIONS:
Superb beaches; the quaint Saint-Louis Museum with local exhibits; a trip out to Langue de Barbarie National Park on a sandy peninsula beside the Atlantic Ocean, with an abundant variety of bird life; The Djoudj National Bird Sanctuary on the southeast bank of the River Senegal, northeast of town – a range of wetland habitats attract around 400 species of bird, the most visible being flamingos and pelicans; the traditional Guet N'Dar fishing community with its rich cultural heritage.

YOU SHOULD KNOW:
Don't plan a quick day trip to Mauretania. Despite being so close to the border, you can't cross at Saint-Louis. The nearest frontier crossing point is actually 100 km (62 mi) upstream. The Saint-Louis Jazz Festival is in May, the city's Blues Festival in January/February.

Cape Coast

WHEN TO GO:
June to September are
favoured months.

TOP FAMILY ATTRACTIONS:
Pristine beaches galore;
exploring Fort William, Fort
Amsterdam and Fort Victoria;
the excellent and well-
organized historical museum
at Cape Coast Castle (one of
Ghana's biggest and most
impressive slave-trade
castles); Cape Coast Centre for
National Culture; a trip out to
Kakum National Park, 30 km
(19 mi) to the south (one of
the best national parks in West
Africa – don't miss the
spectacular canopy walkway);
a short trip to the fishing town
of Elmina with its old town
and Fort Coenraadsburg
(originally built by the
Portuguese in 1555).

YOU SHOULD KNOW:
Vasco da Gama is thought to
have put in here during his
voyage of discovery to India
(with Portuguese traders not
far behind, as usual). The great
American jazz musician Louis
Armstrong believed that his
ancestors were shipped to
America from Cape Coast
Castle.

Cape Coast is a place with a fascinating history. Set around the rocky promontory that protects its bay, the city climbs up steep hills surrounding the centre, with fine colonial architecture dating from the early 1800s as evidence of the city's past. The magnificent Cape Coast Castle, a UNESCO World Heritage Site, looms over crashing waves, a row of black cannons pointing menacingly from the battlements towards non-existent ship-borne enemies.

When Cape Coast was known as Oguaa and already established as a settlement, the Portuguese bought land in the early 1600s and built a castle for their trading post. During the process of periodically changing hands between Sweden, Denmark and the Netherlands, the castle constantly grew. In 1664 it fell to the English and became the administrative centre of the Gold Coast. And so it remained until 1877, when the colony's capital was moved to Accra.

Cape Coast Castle, with its peeling, white-painted exterior, was built to protect timber, ebony and gold trades, but rapidly became an important centre of slaving. This is a deeply moving place. Thousands of slaves languished in dreadful conditions in the dungeons, callously traded for guns, tobacco and beads, before being shipped to the New World. There is an excellent museum in the castle, where guided tours are both illuminating and moving. From either end of the battlements two other historic forts can be seen – in all some 60 forts and trading posts were built along this coast.

Cape Coast was the birthplace of the country's first newspapers, and of the nationalism that finally won its independence. Today it is Ghana's centre of excellence in education and something of a holiday destination, with splendid beaches nearby. It's an ideal location for any visiting family that wants to dodge resort tourism and experience the happier face of this wonderful but often turbulent continent.

*The spectacular canopy
walkway in Kakum
National Park*

Mombasa

Mombasa, Kenya's second city, is East Africa's largest port. Separated from the mainland by two creeks, there is a bridge to the north and a causeway plus railway line to the west. It is only when travelling south by ferry that its island location is really obvious.

Founded by Arab traders during the eighth century, Mombasa was already prosperous when Vasco da Gama visited in 1498. Two years later Portuguese forces arrived, heralding centuries of struggle between the Portuguese and the Shirazi Arabs. In 1840 the Sultan of Zanzibar, who later ceded administration to Britain, seized the town and in 1963 Mombasa became part of newly independent Kenya. This is a Swahili city, although it has a culturally and racially mixed heritage. Its hot, steamy climate informs the pace of life – slow and easy going. This is Kenya's base of coastal tourism – cruise ships and containers dock at Kilindini, the modern harbour, but tourists arriving by train or plane generally head for beaches further north or south (although families who choose the city as their holiday base will not be disappointed).

Mombasa's Old Town is a place of narrow, winding streets and charmingly dilapidated Arab architecture,

featuring carved doorways and fretwork balconies. Overlooking the sea stands Fort Jesus, built by the Portuguese in the 1590s and now an interesting museum. The city's atmosphere is friendly and lively restaurants stay open late. Walking through the Old Town is a sensory pleasure. Everything looks exotic and colourful, people dress in *kangas* and *kikois* – brightly coloured, printed cotton cloths – and the air is heavy with the scent of spice. Visit the Old Harbour, where traditional dhows and other small boats deliver fresh fish and goods from along the coast. The faces, vibrant colours, noise and laughter make Mombasa a stimulating place to visit.

Historic Fort Jesus, listed as a UNESCO World Heritge Site in 2011, was built by the Portuguese in 1593. It is situated at the entrance to the old dhow harbour.

Zanzibar

WHEN TO GO:
September to March
TOP FAMILY ATTRACTIONS:
A serene cruise on an authentic Arab dhow; the House of Wonders, a striking sultan's residence on the seafront, now a museum of Swahili and Zanzibar culture; Palace Museum – the former Omani Sultans' palace now illustrating the lifestyle lived therein; Dr Livingstone's house, actually built for a sultan but inhabited by many Victorian explorers and missionaries; the Nasur Nurmohamed Dispensary – a beautiful old restored building housing the Cultural Centre; a trip out to Jozani Forest-Chwaka Bay, Zanzibar's largest forest area and a haven for wildlife, including the famous Red Colobus monkey (also visit nearby Zanzibar Butterfly Centre).

'Zanzibar' – the word immediately conjures up images of an exotic, distant island, ringed with sparkling, azure seas and impossibly white beaches, the air heavy with the scent of cloves. And Stone Town, the old centre of Zanzibar City, lives up to the dream. Set on a peninsula on the west coast, it is a wondrous blend of Arabic, Indian and African culture and style, with some European influence thrown in for good measure.

For centuries, ships carried spices and slaves between Africa and Asia. Until the late 1800s, Stone Town was ruled by Omani Sultans. As Dar es Salaam and Mombasa gained importance, Stone Town declined. By 1964 the last Sultan had been removed and Zanzibar united with mainland Tanzania. Most of the foreigners left the island, their vacated buildings gradually falling into shabby disrepair. Fortunately, the 21st century has produced renewed interest in

renovating and conserving this quintessentially Swahili heritage.

The Arab Fort, started by Portuguese and finished by Omanis in 1701, is the oldest building here, its high, castellated walls now hiding a green space, shops and a café. The town is littered with gorgeous buildings. Narrow, shadowy paths are lined with Arab houses, plain facades hiding splendid interior courtyards. Long windows are set within deep niches, and first floor walkways enabled Omani women to socialize without being seen in public.

You'll see massive hardwood doors, intricately carved by Indian craftsmen and decorated with Indian-style brass spikes, and beautiful balconies, some original and some added later. Low stone benches in front provide seating for local men, who spend hours there, putting the world to rights. There are so many outstanding buildings to be seen and such a lot of romantic history that the family mustn't be tempted to skip the city in favour of the beach.

The former Ishnashri Dispensary in Stone Town

YOU SHOULD KNOW:
The city's Anglican Cathedral is built on the site of the world's last slave market and the altar sits on the spot where the market's whipping post stood. Freddie Mercury, late great singer with the band Queen, was born in Stone Town – and Mercury's Restaurant near the ferry port is themed and dedicated to his memory. The House of Wonders boasts two firsts – first building in Zanzibar to have electricity, first building in East Africa to have a lift.

Cape Town

South Africa is a great family holiday destination and Cape Town is a wonderful place to start. The city lies beneath Table Mountain, is the capital of Western Cape Province and serves as South Africa's legislative capital. To the other side of the city lies the Cape Peninsula and the two geological features make up the UNESCO World Heritage Site of Table Mountain National Park.

One of the most popular areas in the city is the Victoria and Albert Waterfront, which has hundreds of shops and restaurants. It is also the departure point for trips to the apartheid-era jail on Robben Island and the appealing seal colonies on Duiker and Seal Islands. There are lots of pretty Cape Dutch structures, especially old government buildings in the central business district along Long Street and in Constantia. Long Street has some of the best restaurants in the

Cape Town and the cable car as seen from the top of Table Mountain

country. The British colonial era is reflected in the city hall and the Rhodes Memorial, while the iniquities of apartheid are explored in the District Six Museum, which commemorates residents who were forced to leave when the place was declared a whites-only area.

Because slaves were brought from the Far East, a high proportion of people of south-east Asian heritage live in the city and Bo-Kaap (formerly known as the Malay Quarter) is another popular destination. It has been refurbished and is full of quaint, brightly coloured buildings. The cable car up to the top of Table Mountain is a must (in good weather) and there are tracks leading to the end of the Cape Peninsula. Both areas have fantastic outlooks and an abundance of wildlife. Indeed, there is so much to see and do in Cape Town that any adventurous family will want to return.

A young girl and an African (Jackass) penguin stare at each other on Boulders Beach near Cape Town.

Durban

South Africa's busiest port, Durban was also for many years its most popular tourist destination, although more international tourists now choose to head for Cape Town instead. Even so, the city hasn't mislaid its subtropical climate and stunning beaches, and still makes a great first choice for a relaxing family holiday with all the trimmings. Although Portuguese explorer Vasco da Gama landed in the area in 1493 and named it Natal, Durban's foundations only date back to the 1820s. The large number of Indian workers the British brought here in the 19th century have ensured that Durban has a large population of Asian origin.

Among Durban's most popular tourist spots are the beaches, bars and restaurants of the Golden Mile, the Suncoast Casino, uShaka Marine World – one of the largest aquariums on earth, the African Art Centre, the Maritime Museum and the Botanical Gardens. For those who can face it, the Fitzsimons Snake Park on Lower Marine Parade makes an interesting excursion. Many of the beaches have shark protection nets – shark attacks are not actually as common as all that, but there are Great Whites in the region – and the KZN Sharks Board runs early morning boat trips that allow visitors to watch the staff check the safety gear and, hopefully, spot a variety of marine life.

The large Indian population means that curry is a speciality of the city, especially Bunny Chow – a hollowed out chunk of bread filled with your choice of curry. Wilson's Wharf, off Victoria Embankment, has a wide variety of cuisines, as does Florida Road, which is also great for little boutiques. At the opposite end of the scale, the Gateway Mall is the largest in the southern hemisphere. Tourist Junction is home to good craft shops that sell 'designer-quality' Zulu

WHEN TO GO:
Any time of year (even in winter its warm enough for the beach).
TOP FAMILY ATTRACTIONS:
The Golden Mile – a super-popular stretch of beach-front in the city with wide sands and a warm sea; a must-do trip out to Crocodile Creek in Tongaat, home to over 7,000 Nile crocodiles, alligators, caiman, snakes and other reptiles (also bush and hill trails, waterfall, river plains and thatched buildings with tree-top walkways); the Surfing Museum, cataloguing Durban's eminent place in the annals of surf-riding; for non-surfers, great aqua rides at Waterworld; helicopter sight-seeing flights from Virginia Airport (expensive but memorable); Umgeni River Bird Park with walk-through aviaries, lush vegetation, amazing waterfalls and rock faces, plus a wonderful free-flight show; Phezulu Safari Park out at Bothas Hill.
YOU SHOULD KNOW:
For getting around town safely registered taxis are widely available and relatively inexpensive, but note that they have to be summoned by phone. Brightly coloured 'combi taxis' are everywhere and you hear as well as see them coming (they all have music belting out of powerful speakers), but be sure you know the destination before hopping aboard.

FOLLOWING PAGES:
Durban's Golden Mile   215

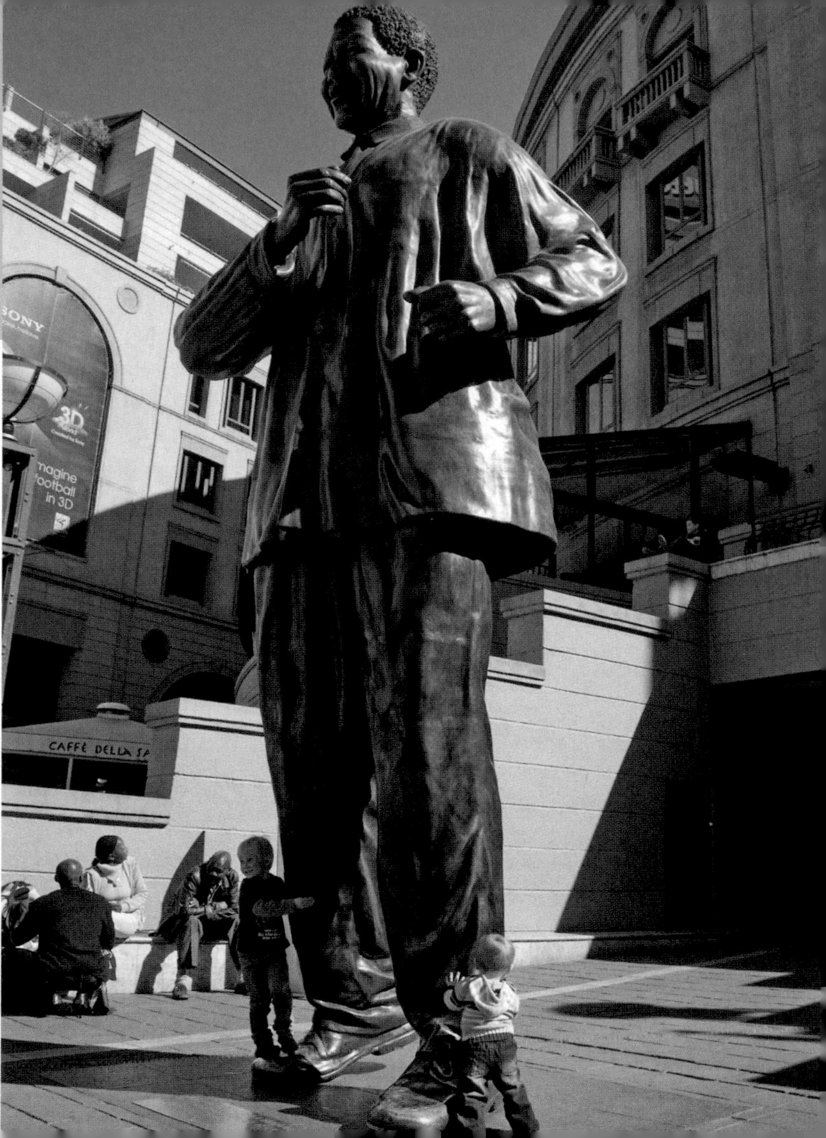
SONY
3D
magine
ootball
in 3D
CAFFÈ DELLA SA

Johannesburg

Established in 1886 as a gold-mining town, South Africa's largest city is the capital of wealthy Gauteng Province. But Johannesburg is not, as is often thought, the country's capital. In fact there are three of those – Pretoria (executive), Bloemfontein (judicial) and Cape Town (legislative) and Jo'burg has never been one of them. The city had a troubled past following the collapse of the apartheid regime and large parts of the city were no-go areas for several years, but this drastic situation is now much improved.

Among the most popular destinations in the city is the Mandela Family Museum in Soweto's Orlando West, while the Apartheid Museum is worth spending an entire day visiting. The art gallery is the biggest on the continent and has both European and African paintings, and the Museum of Africa concentrates more on the region's history and culture, including a large collection of ancient petroglyphs. The more affluent areas of the city are in the north and northwest. Melvilla is particularly well known for its nightlife and bohemian living. Tours of the former townships such as Alexandra and Soweto are becoming increasingly popular.

Of course, the area is rich in wildlife and the Lion Park is where visitors can get up close to lion cubs and drive through an enclosure with prides of adults, as well as antelope, giraffe and zebra. Johannesburg Zoo is the largest in Africa. The Walter Sisulu Botanic Garden is one of the last big green spaces in the city and provides an opportunity to see a wide variety of plants and birds. The Lesedi Cultural Village is home to traditional food and dances of the various cultures of the region - a reminder of the area's past and its rich cultural heritage, which is now being encouraged to flourish once more.

WHEN TO GO:
Any time of year but winters can be cold.
TOP FAMILY ATTRACTIONS:
The Rosebank Rooftop Flea Market every Sunday, atop one of South Africa's best retail shopping malls; Johannesburg Planetarium at the University of the Witwatersrand; Sterkfontein Caves northwest of town, where fossils of early hominids have been found; a trip out to the Rhino and Lion Nature Reserve in Kromdraii, location of the incredible Wonder Cave (the country's third largest); Sci-Bono, Southern Africa's biggest science centre, dedicated to stimulating interest in, enjoyment of and engagement with the wonderful world of science and technology; Gold Reef City, a theme park based around interactive gold-mining experiences (plus thrill rides and other amusements).
YOU SHOULD KNOW:
It may not be one of South Africa's three capitals, but Jo'burg claims to be the lightning capital of the world, so don't be surprised (but do be delighted) if you see a spectacular free light show.

Children play at the feet of the statue of Nelson Mandela in Sandton, north of the city centre.

AUSTRALIA &
NEW ZEALAND

Melbourne

Set around the natural harbour of Port Philip and founded in 1835 as a farming community, Melbourne might have remained a peaceful backwater. But the Victorian gold rush of the 1850s ensured that a rural nowhere became and remained one of Australia's major cities. It was even Australia's capital from the time when the states federated in 1901 until the national Parliament moved to Canberra in 1927.

Melbourne's history can be read in its buildings. The booms of the 1850s, 1880s and early 1970s, its time as national capital and the current period of prosperity have all left their architectural mark, from massive Victorian town halls to the Windsor Hotel and Flinders Street Station, plus modern high-rises of the CBD (Central Business District). Most typical of this mixture of new and old is the tram system on which both heritage and modern trams run.

Like most Australian cities, Melbourne is well provided with parks and is sometimes referred to as Australia's garden city. Carlton Gardens is special, surrounding the Royal Exhibition Buildings built for the international exhibitions of 1880 and 1888. Melbourne also prides itself as Australia's cultural capital, boasting the Melbourne Museum, National Gallery of Victoria (with the largest art collection in the country spread over several buildings) and the Arts Centre Melbourne, which promotes Opera Australia's performances, the Melbourne

Theatre Company and the Melbourne Symphony Orchestra, as well as several theatres in and around the CBD.

Melbourne is probably the most cosmopolitan city in Australia and boasts a large Chinatown with its wide range of mainly Cantonese restaurants, Little Italy and a Greek Precinct for delicious food. The city is justifiably renowned for its different cuisines, from Italian or Greek to Malaysian, Japanese or Thai. There's certainly lots to see and lots to do – and never enough time to see and do it all!

A view of the Melbourne skyline from the Royal Botanical Gardens

Perth sits on the Swan River.

Perth

Perhaps because it is one of the most remote cities on earth, Perth is a lively place that will richly reward any family that makes the necessary expedition. It sits on the Swan River, named after the black swans first seen here by Europeans in the 1690s. Colonists arrived in June 1829 and the settlement became the capital of Western Australia in 1832. However, the city seems much younger than that, because the remaining Victorian buildings are mainly away from the city centre. This is also a city of migrants. About a

quarter of the population was born overseas, creating a fresh, cosmopolitan feel. The lifestyle is largely an outdoor one. There are endless stretches of empty and unspoilt sandy beaches, while people here are barbecue- and sports-crazy.

Inland lies the beautiful winemaking area of the Swan Valley. The first vines were planted here within a year or so of Perth's foundation and this is now one of Australia's premier winemaking locations. The city itself is not over-cultural, but certainly not unendowed. It has the Perth Institute of Contemporary Art, Western Australian Museum, the Art Gallery of Western Australia, Perth Concert Hall and His Majesty's Theatre. Outdoor concerts take place in Subiaco Oval and King's Park, from where sunsets are spectacular. The Perth International Arts Festival is held annually in February and March.

There are also plenty of family-friendly attractions in this vibrant, confident city. All the usual activities associated with an Indian Ocean seaside holiday may be enjoyed, from building sandcastles to parascending, and the Swan River also has areas dedicated to water sports. It's also possible to take a scenic boat trip up to the wine-making region, returning with a bottle or two.

WHEN TO GO:
Any time but red-hot summer (that's December to February), though spring (September to November, when the wildflowers are in bloom) and autumn (March to May) are ideal times to visit.

TOP FAMILY ATTRACTIONS:
Perth Zoo, with over 160 animal species and a wonderful botanical collection; Perth Aquarium and its long underwater tunnel; whale-watching trips run by the Aquarium); surfing at Scarborough Beach (bold beginners welcome); a visit to Rottnest Island and its friendly quokkas (cat-sized marsupials); a trip to the nearby colonial town of Fremantle (don't miss the maritime museum complete with submarine, or historic Fremantle Prison); the delightful Old Mill built in 1835, for a step back in time; Perth Mint tour (gold nuggets galore!); Scitech for fascinating encounters with science and technology; Adventure World out at Bibra Lake, for all the fun of the theme park.

YOU SHOULD KNOW:
The regular afternoon breeze that arrives to cool the city is called the 'Fremantle Doctor' for its relieving effect on a city grilled by the relentless sun. It's possible to take the train to Perth from Sydney via Kalgoorie, Adelaide and Broken Hill. It takes four days and three nights and is one of the world's great railway journeys.

Sydney

Mention of the word Sydney instantly brings to mind views of the iconic Opera House and Harbour Bridge, perhaps illuminated by spectacular fireworks with which the city greets every New Year. But visitors

soon discover there's so much more to see and enjoy, including historic Sydney.

The Rocks, site of the original settlement, has picturesque old buildings. Within easy walking distance are the Harbour Bridge, old Observatory, Garrison Church, Colonial House Museum and

A Koala Bear at Taronga zoo

Cadman's Cottage. Spectacular views over the city can also be obtained from Sydney Tower on Market Street in the central district. Parliament House is in Macquarie Street along with the Sydney Mint and Hyde Park Barracks museums. Beyond is the Domain, home to the Art Gallery of New South Wales, while the Australian Museum is just to the south.

To the north is the best of Sydney's central parks, the Royal Botanic Gardens. It's large enough to lose the family in, although flocks of cockatoos ensure that it is never quiet. At Benelong Point lies Jorn Utzon's Sydney Opera House, a UNESCO World Heritage Site since 2007. Mrs Macquarie's Point is a good place to view it from across the water, but the best photo opportunities are from ferries that criss-cross the harbour. The Darling Harbour area is home to a range of leisure and entertainment possibilities, plus the Powerhouse and Australian National Maritime museums. The city has a wonderfully diverse population and Chinatown is well worth a visit.

Sydney also has around 70 beaches – Bondi the most famous and Manly the most upmarket. Beaches within the harbour are sheltered while those on the ocean have fantastic surf. With its stunning harbourside setting, cliffs overlooking the ocean and surrounding bushland, Sydney is one of the most beautiful, welcoming and energetic cities any family could hope to visit.

A passenger ferry passes beneath the Harbour Bridge with a backdrop of the Opera House and central Sydney.

Auckland

Centred on a narrow isthmus between the Hauraki Gulf and the Tasman Sea, Auckland is a fine city dominated by water and mountains. To the north, Waitemata Harbour is guarded by Rangitoto Island, the youngest of 50 volcanoes and vents that shaped the land hereabouts. With sheltered harbours, easy access to the sea and a strategic location this was an obvious place for settlement and Maori people lived here for nearly 500 years – chiefly on the volcanic heights – before it became established as the capital of New Zealand in 1840 following European settlement, although it kept the title for a mere 25 years. Today, it is a top destination for holidaymakers and never disappoints, whatever their interests.

The western beaches are great for surfers and there are good beaches for swimmers at Devonport, Long Bay and Mission Bay, while the harbours are filled with yachts – this is one of the most popular places in the world for sailors (hence Auckland's nickname as 'The City of Sails'. For landlubbers, the city action is centred around Queen Street, Ponsonby Road and Karangahape Road.

Several of the extinct volcanoes and islands, such as Mount Eden, Waiheke Island and North Head, are natural parks and have remnants of prehistoric settlements and later fortifications. Other popular areas in Auckland's beautiful environs include the Hunua Ranges and the Waiketere Ranges Regional Park. For the culturally inclined Auckland Art Gallery has an important collection of works by New Zealand artists, the Auckland Philharmonic Orchestra is based here and the Auckland Festival is a biennial event featuring local and international music, dance, theatre and visual art. It's not hard to see why Auckland is rated as one of the top ten cities in the world to live in – and that makes it a pretty good family holiday destination, too.

WHEN TO GO:
Any time of year but it can be cold in winter.

TOP FAMILY ATTRACTIONS:
A super-scenic whale and dolphin safari cruise; a jet-boat ride in Waitemata Harbour; Auckland Harbour Bridge (offering high-level walkway for those at least 7 years old and/or bungee jump from 10 years old); amazing views from Sky Tower, the Southern Hemisphere's tallest structure; Auckland Zoo for New Zealand's native animals (and others); Kelly Tarlton's Antarctic Encounter & Underwater World, a unique Pacific and Southern Oceans showcase for a variety of marine life (plus Snowcat rides and penguins!); Rainbow's End, New Zealand's top theme park (great rides including corkscrew rollercoaster).

YOU SHOULD KNOW:
The best way for first-time visitors to see as much as possible of Auckland as quickly as possible is by buying a pass for the easy hop-on hop-off bus service that links all major sites and attractions. It offers unlimited travel complete with audio commentary.

Children enjoying the views of downtown Auckland from the Devonport ferry.

Wellington

An albatross impression at the Royal albatross (wingspan 3.5m/11.5ft) exhibit at Te Papa Tongarewa

The capital of New Zealand since 1865, Wellington is also its cultural hub – renowned for café culture, nightlife and a thriving arts scene. This lively city offers everything required for a great family visit and a great time will be had by all. Wellington sits at the southwestern point of North Island, overlooking the Cook Strait, and is known for the pretty harbour, created by an active geological fault which is causing the land to the west of the harbour to rise up. At the top of the hill is the Botanic Garden, which can be reached on the funicular railway or the exciting Wellington Cable Car from Lambton Quay. The centre of the city is extremely compact, so everything is within easy reach and getting around on foot is a good way to go.

There are all sorts of artistic activities with both professional and community theatres, performances by the New Zealand Symphony Orchestra, the National Opera Company and Royal New Zealand Ballet. There are festivals celebrating almost everything, from the biennial International Festival of the Arts and the annual International Jazz Festival to the New Zealand Affordable Art Show, the Cuba Street Carnival and the World of Wearable Art. Te Papa Tongarewa (Museum of New Zealand) is a must-see among the many museums.

Wellington's café culture is outstanding. Local roasteries produce some of the best coffee in the world and the city also boasts some very fine restaurants, serving everything from Malaysian to Lebanese food and all courses in between. But Wellington isn't really an indoor place. The city sits among wonderful scenery and many visitors venture forth to explore the hills and rugged coastline, encouraged by a network of biking and hiking trails.

royal albatross

233

AMERICAS & THE CARIBBEAN

Montreal

The world renowned Cirque du Soleil

Montreal, the third largest city in Canada and Quebec's biggest, is centred on the island of the same name. The French settled here in 1642 and this heritage is still proudly exhibited today. The city has a cosmopolitan mix of cultures and peoples but retains a distinctly Gallic feel, even though the region came into British possession in 1760. The city's Roman Catholic heritage can be seen in the Basilica of Notre-Dame, St Joseph's Oratory and the Cathedrale Marie-Reine-du-Monde.

Whether exploring historic Old Montreal or sipping a cappuccino at an outdoor café in Little Italy, the energy of this urban playground is contagious. Montreal is divided into neighbourhoods, each representing a unique and lively part of this fabulous, family-friendly city. There is a wide range of museums, including the excellent Museum of Fine Arts in the downtown area. Cultural life centres around the Place des Arts, which is home to the Montreal Symphony Orchestra, l'Orchestre Métropolitan, I Musici de Montreal, the Opera de Montreal and the Grands Ballets Canadiens, as well as several modern dance troupes and the internationally famous Cirque du Soleil. There is also a lively contemporary music

A mother and her daughters at Montreal Insectarium

scene. The Quartier Latin is the place for literature and theatre buffs. The oldest part of the city is Vieux-Montreal with its traditional European flavour – especially in St Denis, which feels like the Left Bank of Paris.

For those who prefer to get away from it all, Parc du Mont-Royal is a beautiful landscaped park on the mountain of the same name, offering a range of outdoor activities and amazing panoramas. Shopping is centred around Saint-Catherine Street but in winter the locals head for the Ville Souterraine, a vast underground area with more than 1,600 shops, 30 cinemas and some 200 restaurants, all sheltered from the harsh winter above.

Quebec City

One of the oldest cities in North America, Quebec has the only surviving walled city north of Mexico, and the historic district of Vieux-Quebec was designated a

Sampling the treats at Choco-Musée Erico.

UNESCO World Heritage Site in 1985 for cultural and historical significance. Its twin areas – Basse-Ville and Haute-Ville – surround the Château Frontenac. In Haute-Ville, you will find narrow lanes running between grey, high-walled houses reminiscent of a medieval French city, while lower down Cap Diamant Basse-Ville – the site of the original settlement – is home to a lively café culture and boutique shops.

The Château Frontenac is one of the city's dominant landmarks – this large hotel on the Cap Diamant looks like a Loire château. The Basilica of Notre-Dame is also very French in feel. Another building left from colonial times is the Haute-Ville's Citadelle, a star-shaped complex of military fortifications. In Basse-Ville you will find the church of Notre-Dame des Victoires. One of the area's best-known attractions is the Musée de la Civilisation.

A wide range of museums cover the history and culture of the region, among them the Musée de Quebec in the Parc des Champs-de-Bataille, which has a first-class art collection. The park is the site of the battle that ended the rule of the French in North America and holds free concerts in summer. At the other end of the year the Quebecois cheer themselves up with the biggest winter carnival in the world, which features a talking snowman called Bonhomme, who inhabits the Snow Palace and presides over horse-drawn sleigh rides, the International Canoe Race across the part-frozen St Lawrence River, dogsled races, parades and the International Snow Sculpture Event. What better way could there be to chase the winter blues away? And if winter fun doesn't appeal, there's a wonderful summer carnival.

WHEN TO GO:
Any time of year, depending on the family's interests, but May to September are the warmest months and it can be very cold in winter.

TOP FAMILY ATTRACTIONS:
Riding the Funiculaire up to the front of the Château Frontenac; a tour of the Old City by horse-drawn carriage; superb city views from the ferry across the St Lawrence Seaway to Lévis; Old Port Interpretation Centre for living history; Canadian Children's Museum for an interactive journey around the world; Choco-musee Erico, a small but tasty chocolate museum; Récréofun Centre d'Amusement, a large family entertainment centre for under-12s; Super Aqua Club, a great water park for all the family (awesome rides!); Méga Parc – located within Les Galeries de la Capitale, it offers 20 attractions including a rollercoaster and skating rink.

YOU SHOULD KNOW:
Quebec comes from the Algonquin word meaning 'where the river narrows'. This is a French-speaking city but English speakers will get by just fine.

*The Château Frontenac
and the Lévis Ferry*

TOP FAMILY ATTRACTIONS:
The view from the top of the
CN Tower (on a clear day!); the
Toronto Islands, once joined to
the mainland, a great spot for
relaxing on lake beaches; Fort
York, dating from 1793;
Ontario Science Centre, with a
variety of science displays that
appeal to children; the famous
Kensington Market; Canada's
Wonderland amusement park
– rides and attractions aplenty,
including animated dinosaurs;
Playdium, an interactive
adventure centre packed with
adrenaline-fuelled games and
activities; Centreville
Amusement Park, just across
the harbour from the city, with
over 30 rides and attractions.

YOU SHOULD KNOW:
In winter Toronto can be prone
to lake-effect snow (which is a
fancy way of saying 'lots of it').
Toronto's Scotiabank
Caribbean Carnival (formerly
Caribana) happens from mid
July to early August and is one
of North America's largest
street festivals.

Toronto

Sitting on the shore of Lake Ontario, Toronto is
Canada's largest city. It consistently rates among the
best places in the world to live (and visit!) and is said
to be the world's most diverse city. The French built a
fort here in 1750, then it was re-established as Fort
York by the British in 1793 before reverting to its old
Native American name in 1834. As well as the long
shorefront onto the lake and large harbour, the city is

intersected by rivers that have created steep gullies that run down towards the shore.

Modern expansion has led to the development of a high proportion of skyscrapers, including the soaring CN Tower. But in the historic Distillery District many old Victorian industrial buildings have been redeveloped to create an area dedicated to culture, shopping, dining and drinking, the arts and entertainment. This is now listed as a national heritage site, while several major museums – including the Art Gallery of Ontario and the Royal

A young boy's hair stands on end with static electricity at the Ontario Science Centre.

Ontario Museum – have had recent facelifts. Other museums include the Bata Shoe Museum and the Gardiner Museum of Ceramic Art. The Don Valley Brick Works has been restored as a heritage centre and park that more than justifies a family visit. Shoppers should head for Yorkville or the Eaton Centre, while for foodies Greektown is a must.

With dozens of music venues and theatres, Toronto

The ever-popular swan ride at Centreville amusement park on Centre Island

is home to two symphony orchestras, numerous dance companies and a handful of opera companies. Annual cultural events include the Canadian National Exhibition and Toronto International Film Festival. There's always something going on, because Toronto is a buzzing multicultural city. But for those who need a breather, there are also wooded ravines where the family can get lost for a couple of hours.

FOLLOWING PAGES: A view of Toronto's skyline and the CN Tower

Vancouver

WHEN TO GO:
Any time of year as the
climate is mild by Canadian
standards, although November
to March sees plenty of rain.
TOP FAMILY ATTRACTIONS:
Beaches in summer; a 45-
minute ferry ride to Vancouver
Island for some of the best
whale-watching in the world;
Grouse Mountain – hike up or
take the Skyride for a stunning
view of the city; Hell's Gate
Airtram across the dramatic
Fraser Canyon (once the site
of a great gold rush);
Vancouver Maritime Museum,

*RIGHT: Walking on Long
Beach at sunset, Pacific
Rim National Park,
Vancouver Island.*

*Whale-watching trips
are very popular.*

One of Canada's fastest growing cities, Vancouver is a
magical place full of contradictions. Named after the
first European to discover the area, George Vancouver,
it is the gateway to the Pacific. Its sheltered harbour
made it an ideal place for settlement, especially after
the discovery of coal nearby led to the need for a port.
Gastown harks back to those days, a quaint Victorian
cobbled enclave now turned from a working port area to
an upmarket home for art galleries, antique shops and
boutiques. Right next to it is the Lookout Tower, an
observation deck 33 floors above the Harbour Centre. A
different range of views can be obtained from Stanley
Park, a vast area of woodland, lakes and gardens.

Vancouver is renowned for its easy-going,
cosmopolitan lifestyle, with leisure activities including
sailing and trips into the surrounding wilderness in
summer and skiing in winter. A long history as a port
has created communities from a wide range of

backgrounds and Chinatown is one of the largest in North America – a must for atmosphere, shops and restaurants. World cuisine is also a speciality of the city, featuring (among others) Indian, Italian, Greek, Japanese and Korean food in the respective quarters, while Gastown is home to world-class restaurants.

Culture is centred on Granville Island, which is home to both traditional arts centres and events and the city's sometimes wild nightlife. But by day it is the site of a vast public market the family will find fascinating. The city's museums include the Museum of Anthropology and the Vancouver Art Gallery, housed in a beautiful Edwardian building. This vibrant city is set at the edge of the Pacific Ocean and, with its mix of old and new, high culture and alternative bands, urban living and beautiful wilderness, has to be on every family's list of places to visit.

FOLLOWING PAGES:
Downtown Vancouver
at night

including a Children's Discovery Centre and boats in Heritage Harbour; Stanley Park's amazing Vancouver Aquarium with over 160 aquatic displays, including a dolphin show; Telus World of Science, a science centre at the end of False Creek featuring interactive exhibits and displays; Playland in Hastings Park – Canada's oldest theme park, but still licensed to thrill.

YOU SHOULD KNOW:
Getting around town isn't hard – after San Francisco, Vancouver has the second-largest trolleybus fleet in North America. Vancouver is third only to Hollywood and New York as a North American film production centre.

249

Charleston

On the Atlantic coast of South Carolina, Charleston was originally a walled city and home to two forts with pivotal roles in America's history. Fort Moultrie withstood the British in the Revolutionary Wars and Fort Sumter saw the first shot fired in the American Civil War. The only part of the original walls to remain is the Powder Magazine. Its site on a peninsula between the Ashley and Cooper rivers made it an ideal defensive location and the blockade of Charleston's port was a not-always-successful part of the North's strategy during the American Civil War. That port is still among the busiest in the world.

The downtown area is home to the central business district and many cultural and historic sites. Revenue from surrounding plantations made the city rich. Surviving buildings from that era include St Michael's Episcopal Church, the Old Exchange and Customs House (scene of the ratification of the US Constitution in 1788), the City Hall and the County Court House. There are also many pretty houses in 'historic Charleston', the epitome of Southern colonial charm. Rainbow Row by the waterfront has pastel-coloured historic homes.

In some ways similar to New Orleans, Charleston's culture is a mixture of French, West African and traditional American South. French influence can be seen in the dainty red-and-white Huguenot church. The area's plantation past can be seen in the Boone Hall and Magnolia Plantations, Drayton Hall and Middleton Place, while Charleston Museum was the first museum in America and the Gibbes Museum holds more than 10,000 works of art. There are many other museums and historical attractions lurking around almost every corner. Each district of the city has its own unique character and charm to fascinate the family, with numerous gardens and parks to chill out in should sight-seeing fatigue strike.

USS Yorktown *is now a visitor attraction at Patriot's Point.*

Rest those feet and enjoy a horse-drawn carriage tour!

Los Angeles

The 'City of Angels' is indivisible from the film
industry and it's not only visitors who flock to the
glitzy home of the American movie business. Almost
everyone appears to be an aspiring actor and this is a
city full of beautiful people. Also associated with the
California beach and surf lifestyle and music of the
1960s and the urban rap and hard rock of the 1980s
and 1990s, Los Angeles remains a hotbed of live
music performances and lively
street culture.

Over time the city has
engulfed smaller
neighbourhoods, although
many of these – such as
Chinatown and Little Tokyo –
retain their own character,
while farther out the wealthy
enclaves of Venice Beach, Bel-
Air, Beverley Hills and Pacific
Pallisades are fun places to
take a peek through the gates
of the rich and famous. Iconic
locations include Graumann's
Chinese Theatre and the
Hollywood Walk of Fame,
idiosyncratic Watts Towers or
film studios when they are
open for tours. Overseas
sports fans should head for
Dodger Stadium for baseball
or to the Staples Center for a
basketball game featuring the
legendary LA Lakers.

Naturally, shopping is a
way of life for many here, and
Rodeo Drive in Beverley Hills

is a must, if only to press noses to windows. Other tempting targets include the now cleaned-up Sunset Strip or Hollywood Boulevard. In fact, there are plenty of other rewarding places to see and things to do, but it would be a shame to visit LA and miss out on all that glamour. But if the frenetic pace of life in one of the world's largest conurbations gets a bit much, head for the beach or take a trip into the surrounding hills to recharge the family's batteries.

FOLLOWING PAGES: Cycling at Venice Beach.

Mickey and the gang at Disneyland, Anaheim

Miami

Towards the south of Florida, and gateway to both the famous Everglades and the Florida Keys, Miami is one of the fastest-growing cities in America, with a skyline fast rivalling those of Chicago and New York. With a large proportion of residents from Central and South America, plus a huge Cuban contingent, Latin music rings through the air and Miami is regarded as one of the liveliest cities in the world. With glorious weather, this is a great place for the family to relax.

Miami's unique cultural mix means that it also has a special food heritage and is home to 'Nuevo Latino', a mix of Caribbean, Latin American and European cooking styles using local produce. This is also known as Florribean. A more poignant monument to people who have come here looking for a new life is the Freedom Tower. Once newspaper offices, it later became a processing centre for the seemingly never-ending flood of refugees from Cuba and now has a small museum about their life in America. It also just happens to be a beautiful building.

Contrary to popular belief it does rain here, and wet days are ideal to visit one or more of Miami's many visitor attractions, some cultural and some fully orientated towards pure entertainment. However you play it, Miami is definitely not a place for families who want a quiet, relaxing holiday in the sun. Going to the beach is more about seeing and being seen than about sunbathing. There are almost as many aspiring models and actors here as in Los Angeles. However, Miami's sheer vibrancy and joie de vivre make it a place the whole family will enjoy.

WHEN TO GO:
Spring, autumn or winter (the summer months of June to September are the hottest, wettest and most humid).

TOP FAMILY ATTRACTIONS:
Beaches and water sports (especially in Miami Beach); vibrant Hispanic culture in Little Havana; Miami Science Museum and Planetarium; the Miami Children's Museum – play, learn, imagine and create!; Jungle Island with animals, birds, walking trails and shows; the Seaquarium, a must for dolphin lovers; Zoo Miami for over 1,200 wild animals (including exotic species) in a free-range environment; a day trip to Key West.

YOU SHOULD KNOW:
Metrorail is an elevated rail line that connects many areas of tourist interest and a network of bus routes allows visitors to get almost anywhere in the sprawling Miami metro area without a car. The Ancient Spanish Monastery was originally built in 12th-century Spain, but tycoon William Randolph Hearst bought it for his California estate. It never got there, remaining in New York Harbour until 1954 when it was shipped to Miami and rebuilt.

The Killer whale show at Seaquarium, Key Biscayne

New York City

The Manhattan skyline as seen from the Liberty Island Ferry

New York's five boroughs – Brooklyn, the Bronx, Manhattan, Queens and Staten Island – and its surrounding metropolitan area make up one of the world's largest cities. It would be possible to holiday here for a year and merely scratch the surface of a city that is home to some of the world's best museums, great tourist attractions, entertainment unlimited and fantastic food, with life lived at frantic pace by one of the most energetic and culturally diverse populations imaginable.

First visited by Europeans in 1524, settled as New Amsterdam in 1614 and renamed New York after being captured by the British, this great city has long been one of the most important in the United States. Its harbour has seen the arrival of millions of immigrants, welcomed from 1866 by the iconic Statue of Liberty. Their history is recorded at the moving Immigration Museum on Ellis Island. Other famous sights are Brooklyn Bridge, the Empire State Building, United Nations building, Rockefeller Center and the interior of Grand Central Station.

Shopping is a way of life and must-visits include Macy's, Bloomingdale's, Tiffany's, Chinatown, SoHo, Greenwich Village and the meatpacking district, although this is just the tip of the iceberg. Greenwich Village, SoHo and the East Village are full of character, as are Little Italy and Chinatown. Museums include the Cloisters on Manhattan Island, Brooklyn Museum of Art, the Museum of

Modern Art, the Frick Collection, Metropolitan Museum of Art, Solomon R. Guggenheim Museum and Pierpoint Morgan Library, which between them could keep culture lovers busy for weeks. And that's before tackling Broadway's hit shows, off-Broadway innovation and classical music at Carnegie Hall, the Lincoln Center or the New York State Theater. Indeed, the problem for visitors is not so much what to do as what has been missed when time in this turbo-charged city runs out.

LEFT: The Empire State Building from Rockefeller Centre, Manhattan

The American Museum of Natural History

Orlando

It was already a centre for citrus production and a popular resort, but the great Florida Land Boom of the 1920s saw the city of Orlando in Central Florida expand rapidly for a place that had seen its first European settler barely 80 years before. But all that came to an end when a series of hurricanes hit Florida at the end of the decade, swiftly followed by The Great Depression. Nonetheless, the place nicknamed 'The City Beautiful' continued to grow steadily. But it was only in the mid 1960s, with the announcement that Walt Disney World would be built nearby, that Orlando found its true metier as the fun capital of the USA.

Since then this pleasant city with a semi-tropical climate has boomed, becoming a magnet for invading

armies of native-born Americans and foreign tourists and America's favourite family holiday destination by far. Tourism is a mainstay of the city's economy, but Orlando is also a major centre for defence and hi-tech industries and a national player on the commercially important convention circuit, the Orange County Convention Centre being the second-largest such facility in the USA. The city itself has a relatively small population, but sits in the middle of a metropolitan area with a much larger one.

This sprawling conurbation has little of particular architectural or cultural distinction, although the downtown area has the usual high-rises towering above the flatlands and there are several theatres. This is an area richly endowed with lakes, including beautiful Lake Eola in Downtown Orlando, complete with the famous fountain that serves as a symbol of the city. There are several vast malls for power shoppers, but the real attraction for all those visiting families is not shopping, or the city itself, but all those fabulous amusement parks along International Drive.

LEFT: The Wizarding World of Harry Potter at Universal Studios

Feeding the dolphins at SeaWorld.

Seattle

The Museum of Flight

*RIGHT: Children on a ride
at the Seattle Center with
the Space Needle in the
background.*

There is evidence of settlement here since the end of the last Ice Age, but Seattle on the USA's north-western coast was not reached by Europeans until the 1850s. Thereafter it became a trading port, an important centre for the lucrative logging industry and – in the last years of the 19th century – a centre for onward transit of the men with dreams of untold riches and supplies to sustain them, all heading north to the Klondike gold fields. Nowadays, hi-tech is the name of the game.

Visitors love Seattle's wonderful setting amid spectacular coastal and mountain scenery, earning its tag 'The Emerald City'. On the coast of Puget Sound and backed by the Cascade Range, notably Mount Rainier, Seattle has a reputation for always being wet. But this is undeserved – the place can sometimes seem grey, and Puget Sound is frequently engulfed in fog, but actually Seattle gets less rain than many other American cities. The soaring modern skyline is dominated by numerous tall buildings, including the

ENTRANCE

Playing in a fountain at the Seattle Center.

76-storey Columbia Center, the Smith Tower, the Washington Mutual Tower and the Space Needle.

Seattle is well known for its flourishing arts scene, from the Seattle Symphony Orchestra to modern music in all its forms. The city's theatres also host a wide range of performance poetry, including the Seattle Poetry Slam, plus quirky fringe events. Other happenings include the annual Seattle International Film Festival and the Greek Festival. Visual arts are catered for in the Henry Art Gallery, Seattle Art Museum, Frye Art Museum, Seattle Asian Art Museum and many smaller contemporary galleries.

But visiting families should find time for outdoor activities or simply having fun. As well as providing a beautiful backdrop to the city, the Cascades are popular for hiking and skiing, while Puget Sound is a magnet for water-sporters. And non-active types are not left out, for Seattle offers plenty of other entertainment.

St Louis

Among the nicknames with which St Louis is tagged are 'The Gateway City' and 'Gateway to the West'. These perfectly describe the location, situated as it is where the pioneering Oregon Trail met the Missouri. It sits near the confluence of the Mississippi and Missouri rivers and became a significant river port when steamboats were an important means of transport. It is also where Lewis and Clark set off from on their expedition to find an overland route to the Pacific, an epic two-and-a-half-year return trip which is among themes explored in the city's Missouri History Museum. Today, the city is a thoroughly modern destination with much to offer holidaymakers.

St Louis has splendid architecture old and new, including the Basilica of St Louis, King of France and St Louis Abbey. Union Station is a destination in itself, the Fox Theatre on Grand Boulevard is special and there are beautiful mansions in such areas as Hortense Place. The Pulitzer Foundation for the Arts is located in a building which is worth a visit on its own merit, while St Louis Art Museum has a large range of both ancient artefacts and modern art. The Riverfront area, especially to the north of the Eads Bridge, is famous for its eateries while the Hill is the best place to go for the area's renowned Italian food.

Forest Park is an essential port of call for visitors – even larger than New York's Central Park, it is home to the zoo, Municipal Theatre, Science Center and the Art Museum. Perhaps the most iconic place in St Louis is the Jefferson National Expansion Memorial, which commemorates westward expansion of the United States. The stainless steel Gateway Arch was designed by Eero Saarinen and is one of the city's most popular attractions.

WHEN TO GO:
Any time, but this is a wet (and sometimes cold) place that is subject to storms at any time. July and August are very hot, January and February are very cold.

TOP FAMILY ATTRACTIONS:
Riverboat cruises; Cahokia Mounds in Collinsville – the site of one of the largest pre-Columbian cities north of Mexico; the vast Forest Park for a huge range of outdoor activities; the Missouri Botanical Garden with its amazing Climatron dome; a ride to the top of Gateway Arch, the tallest man-made monument in the United States; the Museum of Transportation in Kirkwood for planes, trains and automobiles; St Louis Zoo, one of the best in America (includes petting zoo); St Louis Science Center, promising fun for all the family; the Magic House, a captivating children's museum; a shortish trip out to the Six Flags amusement park.

YOU SHOULD KNOW:
It is said that St Louis is second only to Washington DC when it comes to free activities on offer. The Eads Bridge was the first to cross the Mississippi River, back in 1874, and was then the world's longest. The Mardi Gras festival in the old French quarter of Soulard is America's second largest (after New Orleans).

FOLLOWING PAGES: The St Louis skyline and the Gateway Arch reflected in the Mississippi River at sunset.

Washington

There are many cities worth visiting in the USA, but Washington DC is both a world-class metropolis and one of the most interesting. The nation's capital sits between Maryland and Virginia and houses some of the most iconic buildings and monuments in America. It also has many charming areas and some of the best museums on the planet. Be prepared for a lot of walking!

The National Mall is an area of parkland which joins the White House and the buildings of the Capitol. At its heart is the Washington Monument, while the Vietnam Veterans Memorial is in nearby Constitution Gardens. Other monuments include the Lincoln Memorial, Franklin Delano Roosevelt Memorial, Korean War Veterans Memorial and United States Navy Memorial.

The must-visit Smithsonian Institution is a vast collection of museums, including the National Air and

A family explores the Smithsonian American Art Museum.

Space Museum, Smithsonian American Art Museum, the National Museum of Natural History, National Portrait Gallery, National Museum of the American Indian and more. Among Washington's historic districts, Georgetown is worth an especial mention for its pretty brick town houses and cobbled streets. It is a good place for fine dining and upmarket boutique shops. The Adams Morgan district is another good area to head for, with a wide variety of places to eat. The Potomac River waterfront is also interesting.

Among the green areas of the city are the US National Arboretum, Rock Creek Park, Theodore Roosevelt Island and the areas near the Potomac River, especially the Potomac Gorge. After

years of work, the latter is now once again providing a breeding ground for America's national bird, the Bald Eagle. Arlington National Cemetery, just across the border in Virginia, is the moving resting place of tens of thousands of Americans, from casualties of the American Revolutionary Wars onwards, as well as explorers, astronauts, writers and presidents.

The awe-inspiring Thomas Jefferson Memorial

FOLLOWING PAGES:
The amazing dinosaur skeletons at the National Museum of Natural History

Santo Domingo de Guzmán Church is famous for its decoration both inside and out. The elaborate altar is made of gold and beautifully carved wood.

WHEN TO GO:
Any time of year
TOP FAMILY ATTRACTIONS:
Beaches, beaches and beaches; the historic centre with pedestrian streets and long-established Llano Park; Mercado Benito Juárez for an authentic slice of Mexican market life (and just about anything you need to buy); the Ethnobotanical Garden around the former monastery of Santo Domingo; Teotitlan del Valle

Oaxaca

Oaxaca is a lovely city on the Pacific coast with stunning sandy beaches for swimming, sunbathing and surfing, lapped by gorgeous green sea. It is renowned for being a peaceful and welcoming place for a relaxed family holiday. This area was long a centre for pre-Columbian peoples and some of the most important ruins from that era lie high in the mountains above the city. Together with the city's historic centre they make up the UNESCO World Heritage Site of the Historic Centre of Oaxaca and Archaeological Site of Monte Albán. Native American culture and traditions are much more in evidence here than in other parts of the country. The Day of the Dead celebrations are reputed to be the best in Mexico.

The Conquistador Hernán Cortés annexed this scenic area as his personal property, but subsequent earthquakes mean that little evidence of the early Spanish colonial period remains, although there are plenty of fine buildings constructed in the 18th century. Like so many cities in Mexico, Oaxaca has a large number of religious buildings including the Cathedral de Oaxaca, Santo Domingo de Guzmán (the convent buildings of which house a museum of Oaxacan life), the Basilica de la Soledad, San Felipe Neri and San Juan de Dios (finished in 1703). Other museums the family should find fascinating include the Rufino Tamayo Museum, which specializes in pre-Columbian art and the Museum of Contemporary Art.

The historic old city is a lovely place with colonial architecture and numerous plazas, courtyards and narrow streets, including the central square, the Zócalo. Most of the important buildings are within easy reach on foot. Oaxaca is renowned for two drinks — hot chocolate and alcoholic Mezcal – and the food here is great, with lots of restaurants specializing in seafood. The kids will be delighted (or horrified) by the fact that local dishes include *chapulines* (grasshoppers).

village for its wonderful woven fabrics and ethnic artefacts; a trip to the Zapotec ruins of Monte Albán.

YOU SHOULD KNOW:
The Day of the Dead Festival in early November or the month-long Guelaguetza Festival in July are great times to visit Oaxaca. Best not to follow the signs for Zipolite – it's a nudist beach. Arbol del Tuleis is the tree with the world's largest base, said to be 1,400 years old (located off the Oaxaca-Mitla road).

The pre-Columbian site of Monte Albán

Panama City

WHEN TO GO:
Any time (but be aware that it's hot all year).
TOP FAMILY ATTRACTIONS:
The sensational view over city and sea from Ancon Hill; a boat trip along the canal – a 77-km (48-mi) journey from one end to the other, taking in stunning scenery and such landmarks as the Bridge of the Americas (or do the same journey by train); Miraflores Lock visitor centre; Las Bóvedas, a waterfront promenade jutting into the Pacific; assorted tourist attractions at the Amador Causeway adjacent to the canal entrance; MARTA, the Museo Antropológico with fascinating exhibits charting Panama's ancient past; Summit Botanical Gardens complete with small zoo.
YOU SHOULD KNOW:
Panama City was the starting point for Spanish expeditions that conquered the Inca Empire and most of the gold and silver Spain looted from the Americas passed through on its way to Europe. The city is increasingly becoming a retirement destination for Americans, who find their dollars stretch much further in this welcoming city.

Located at the Pacific end of the Panama Canal, Panama City was founded in 1519 by Pedro Arias de Avila, destroyed by fire in the 17th century after a dramatic surprise attack by the pirate Henry Morgan and subsequently rebuilt a few miles away. It became the national capital of this small nation in 1903. The completion of the canal in 1914 led to exponential growth, although it would be many decades before Panama actually gained control of its lucrative strategic asset from the USA.

The ruins of the old city form a UNESCO World Heritage Site, which was inscribed in 1997. The city and its surrounds provide an interesting if slightly unusual destination for a family holiday with much to see and do. Panama City has a soaring modern skyline but the city is surrounded by a large belt of tropical rainforest. Ironically, modern development (the canal) has actually saved the rainforest, which is essential to ensure that the canal doesn't run dry.

Even before construction of the canal joining two oceans, Panama was an important gateway between the Pacific and the Caribbean because it was the shortest land crossing, and thus became an important commercial and trading centre. The old quarter of the city – Casco Viejo – has the best of the old architecture, including the cathedral. The modern city

A view of Casco Viejo –
Panama City's old quarter

is developing rapidly, with a high proportion of
skyscrapers. The former canal zone, once out of
bounds to non-Americans, is fast becoming a tourist
destination in itself. The city's nightlife, museums,
shopping and culture can rival any in Central or
South America. Right on the doorstep is the rich
rainforest, and the Parque Metropolitano beside the
canal has a wide range of wildlife including puma,
alligators, tapir, sloths, toucans and monkeys to
marvel over.

281

Havana

WHEN TO GO:
Any time (it's hot but not
unpleasantly so all year).
TOP FAMILY ATTRACTIONS:
Beautiful beaches; the
Hemingway Museum in his
former home, documenting the
author's turbulent life and
works; Castillo de La Real
Fuerza, the oldest walled
fortress in the New World, now
a great maritime museum;
surprisingly unghoulish –
Necrópolis Cristóbal Colón, a
famous cemetery and an open-
air museum; the Jardin
Zoologico, an old-fashioned
zoo in the Vedado area; the
National Aquarium for tropical
fish and a dolphin show; a trip
out of town to the huge
Parque Lenin with many
attractions, including an
aquarium and scenic narrow-
gauge railway.
YOU SHOULD KNOW:
Ironically, the Museum of the
Revolution is in an opulent
building that was formerly the
Presidential Palace of
overthrown Juan Batista, now
housing such items as Fidel
Castro's boat and the clothing
worn by revolutionary hero
Che Guevara when he was
killed. Che didn't hate all things
American – his 1960 Chevrolet
is in the Automobile Museum.

*FOLLOWING PAGES: Plaza
de la Catedral
buzzes with tourists
and vendors.*

*RIGHT: A classic
American car parked in
front of the Art Nouveau
Capitolio depicts
perfectly the vibrant
and eclectic style
of Cuba.*

As Cuba increasingly opens up to the outside world, its enchanting capital city provides a great place for a family holiday – and the only place in the world where it's still possible to charge round the streets in an unofficial taxi that's a 1950s American car. Havana is the island's largest and most beautiful city. Although its architectural splendour is somewhat faded, it has colonial buildings from succeeding centuries – defensive walls and the fortress of El Morro, grand neoclassical houses in French or Spanish style, neo-Baroque buildings such as the German-style Gran Teatro, the Art Nouveau Capitolio and Art Deco Edificio Bacardi.

The importance of the old city (Habana Vieja) was recognized in 1982 when it gained UNESCO World Heritage status. But Cuba's political isolation ensured that historic areas have not been invaded by fast-food chains or identikit coffee shops. In some places, dilapidation crosses from the picturesque to the pitiful, but even then it manages to be photogenic. Government-funded restoration programmes are successfully bringing some buildings back into use without ruining their character.

The city's links with and importance to the region's trade with Europe are evident in the many treasures in around 50 wonderful museums, including many dedicated to fine arts, Afro-Caribbean religious artefacts and Arabic and Asian arts. The must-see museums, however, are the Museum of the Revolution and the Hemingway Museum. But Havana is not just about its beautiful buildings and cultural opportunities. This city and its people have a vibrant character, as you would expect from a nation whose national drinks are rum, daiquiris and the mojito and whose national dance is the samba. Even though poor in material terms, Havana's five centuries of existence have made it rich in history, music, culture and food.

Kingston

Set on a protected harbour on the southeast coast of Jamaica, Kingston was founded in the 1690s after an earthquake destroyed the nearby roistering pirate haven of Port Royal. The city has been ravaged by other earthquakes and fires since, but is still a joyous place for any family to visit. The sound of reggae fills the air in this laid-back city by the sea and the people are super-friendly.

Spanish Town in the west of the city was the capital for some two centuries and its surviving old buildings include St James' Cathedral and the Old King's House, among a mix of Spanish-style and Georgian architecture. The Jamaican People's Museum of Crafts and Technology is also here, and the Town Square has a lively

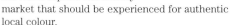

market that should be experienced for authentic local colour.

The dilapidated old waterfront area of the city has been redeveloped into a modern, spacious commercial area with wide boulevards and open spaces. The National Gallery is in the Kingston Mall on Ocean Boulevard and is devoted to the works of Jamaica's best artists while the most famous museum of all is, of course, that dedicated to reggae's great Bob Marley in his former home on Hope Road.

New Kingston is where the new upmarket areas and shopping malls are, but the downtown area gives a real feel of the city (although it should be avoided at night) with brightly coloured buildings and people who mostly live their lives in the open. North of New Kingston are the really rich areas with magnificent houses to marvel at, against the stunning backdrop of the Blue Mountains. If the colour and noise gets too much, head for the offshore beaches of Lime Cay or Hellshire, or up into the Blue Mountains themselves.

The Bob Marley Museum is in his former home.

Quito

San Francisco de Quito lies in a verdant valley on the slopes of the Pichincha volcano, some 25 km (16 mi) south of the equator. At a height of 2,850 m (8,698 ft), making it the second highest capital city in the world (after La Paz in Bolivia), Quito lies amid the Andes in a truly awesome setting. Its name means 'centre of the world' in the language of the Tsáchila, some of the first people to have settled in this part of Ecuador, and this city in the clouds makes a special holiday destination.

Quito is divided into two parts. The Old City is the heritage district situated to the north, while further south the New City boasts modern architecture, broad avenues and urban parks. The Old City contains a wealth of historical buildings, the New City is home to a wide variety of restaurants, cinemas and nightclubs. The centre of the Old City became the first UNESCO World Heritage Cultural Site in 1978 and is renowned for colonial architecture. The most impressive example of this is the Government Palace, a mixture of Spanish and Moorish architecture. El Ejido is the park situated between the

old part of the city and the modern section. Here local handicrafts are sold every weekend.

Aside from its superlative setting, a major part of the charm of Quito lies in its numerous open spaces. Parque Metropolitano, located in the north of the city, is one of the largest urban parks in South America. It offers trails through eucalyptus forest, ample picnic areas and many sculptures. La Carolina park is where the locals hang out. Lying in the middle of the business and shopping district, it provides a good focal point for the city. The park also contains the Quito Exhibition Centre and Botanical Gardens.

The Church of San Francisco in the Plaza de San Francisco

A view of the famous ruins of Machu Picchu

Cusco

Cusco is a high-altitude city in southeastern Peru that will provide interested families with incomparable insight into Inca culture. South America's oldest continuously inhabited city, it is located near the Urubamba Valley (Sacred Valley) of the Andes Mountain range. Cusco was officially founded in 1534 by the Spanish conquistador Francisco Pizarro, although its history goes back much further. Legend has it that in the 12th century the first Inca, Manco Capac, 'son of the sun', was charged by Inti the sun god to find 'qosq'o' (the navel of the earth). Descendants argue that it was he who founded the

city that was to become the thriving capital of the western hemisphere's greatest empire.

After the Inca city was sacked, the Spanish undertook construction of a new city on the foundations of the old, replacing temples with churches and palaces with colonial mansions. However, an earthquake in 1950 destroyed many Spanish colonial buildings, while the city's Inca structures withstood the quake. The mixed architecture, the remaining Palace of the Incas, Temple of the Sun, Temple of the Virgins – together with Quechua-speaking Incan descendents crowding Cusco's stone-walled streets in traditional clothing – are all testament to the enduring legacy of the Inca Empire.

Make a day trip to the amazing Inca city ruins of Machu Picchu, accessible by foot on the Inca trail or by train (although access is now restricted), plus the fortresses of Ollantaytambo and Sacsayhuaman. Or simply stay in the city and visit Cusco's Cathedral, a fabulous repository of colonial art. The cathedral is combined with El Triunto (1536), the oldest church in Cusco, to its right, and the church of Jesus Maria (1733) positioned to its left. The main structure is on the site of Inca Viracocha's Palace, and was built using blocks pilfered from the site of Sacsayhuaman.

WHEN TO GO:
Any time (hot but not unpleasantly so all year round, with a dry season from April to October).

TOP FAMILY ATTRACTIONS:
Riding the luxurious Hiram Bingham train to Machu Picchu; Museo Inka, with a collection of Inca mummies in a splendid colonial mansion; Museo de Arte Religioso, housed in a handsome colonial palace; San Blas Church, with an ornate pulpit considered one of the jewels of colonial art in the Americas; the combined sacred sites of the Temple of the Sun at Koricancha and the Convent of Santo Domingo; the chocolate museum and manufactory, also cocoa farm tours and chocolate workshops; Cusco Planetarium for insight into the relationship of the Andean people with the heavens.

YOU SHOULD KNOW:
The alternative name of the city (often used) is Cuzco. In 2006 this historic capital of the sun-worshipping Inca Empire was declared to be the city with the highest UV light level on earth (so keep putting on the sun block). The air is thin and even minor exertion can lead to breathlessness (until acclimatized).

Brasilia

Designed from the start to be Brazil's capital and promote colonization of the country's interior, Brasilia's original construction started in 1956 and the new city in the central highlands was officially inaugurated just 41 months later in April 1960. The principal urban planner was Lúcio Costa and the lead architect was Oscar Niemeyer. Brasilia was listed as a UNESCO World Heritage Site in 1987, and any families that have tasted Rio's hedonistic pleasures will find that a visit to Brasilia shows a very different –

The striking interior of Catedral Metropolitana where three sculptures of angels are suspended by steel cables.

and interesting – side of a vast country heading at full speed for major-nation status. This is a masterpiece of modernist architecture and the only world city that didn't even exist in the mid-20th century.

The basic layout of this modern city is cruciform and from the air Brasilia is variously described as looking like an aeroplane or a butterfly. It is possible to mention only a few of the city's iconic buildings here: The Palácio da Alvorada, the official presidential residence, the National Congress, the Complexo Cultural da República on the Monumental Axis and the more recent Juscelino Kubitschek bridge over Lake

Paranoá are among the highlights. However, the building considered by most to be the best in town is the amazing Catedral Metropolitana. Also built by Niemeyer, the circular hyperboloidal structure was designed to represent a pair of hands praying.

The soaring television tower is the spot to head for to get an overview of the city, while the Ermida Dom Bosco offers views across Lake Paranoá and gorgeous sunsets. Other open spaces include the Parque da Cidade and Brasilia National Park. Don't expect amusement parks and tourist entertainments. This young city, filled with stunning modernist architecture and public art, is a must-see for its own sake.

WHEN TO GO:
Any time of year (but it can get quite hot in September and October, while May and June are the preferred months).
TOP FAMILY ATTRACTIONS:
A Brasilia tour that takes in the city's main architectural sights; the interior of the cathedral with its stunning glasswork; the Historical Museum of Brasilia in the Praça dos Três Poderes (Square of the Three Powers); Brasilia National Park for local flora and fauna plus natural swimming pools; Parque Rogério Phyton Farias, the largest urban park in Brazil with woods and numerous recreational areas; Poço Azul waterfall, forming beautiful pools in quartz rock; picnics beside, and water sports on, Lake Paranoá; the Zoological and Botanical Garden, with a lake and theatre; President Médici Sports Center, a facility including everything from a car racing circuit to a swimming pool and children's playground.
YOU SHOULD KNOW.
Despite Brasilia's ultra-modern image, there is a thriving flea market at the base of the Television Tower every Sunday and a number of stalls specializing in local crafts and souvenirs are open there all week.

Sucre

WHEN TO GO:
Any time (the climate is very agreeable).

TOP FAMILY ATTRACTIONS:
Casa de la Libertad, a historical museum in a former convent where Bolivian independence was declared; a guided tour of Cal Orck'o Dinosaur Tracks (the Dino Truck leaves thrice daily from the corner of Plaza 25 de Mayo); the best view in town from the Café Mirador, attached to the children's Museo De Los Niños Tanga-Tanga; the Inca Pallay, a weavers' and artisans' cooperative where you can buy intricately woven textiles and see weavers at work; Iglesia de la Merced for one of the finest church interiors in the country, including filigree and gold-inlay pulpit and Baroque-style altar; a visit to the extraordinary 19th-century La Glorieta Castle.

YOU SHOULD KNOW:
The Fiesta de Chu'tillos at the end of August features folk dancing from all over South America.

Known as the 'Cradle of Liberty', this is the place where Bolivian independence was declared in 1825. In a valley surrounded by low mountains in the central highlands at an altitude of 2,800 m (9,184 ft), Sucre is Bolivia's most beautiful and tranquil city, with a wealth of colonial architecture, flower-filled courtyards, dainty patios and proud, law-abiding citizens. It was built with wealth generated by nearby silver mines.

The 16th-century Renaissance Cathedral on Plaza de Maya has a landmark bell tower and the museum next door contains a fascinating collection of religious relics. At the Convento de San Felipe Neri you can climb to the top for stunning vistas over the 'White City of the Americas'. The monks used to meditate up here on the roof terraces as the scent of roses drifted up from the courtyards below.

The climate in Sucre is comfortably mild and it's an easy place to visit and enjoy. It has become a fashionable destination for students of Spanish and the university has the reputation of being the centre of progressive thought within the country. But it may be necessary to keep youngsters on a leash – this is also Bolivia's chocolate capital, with chocolate shops (many of which offer free tastings) on every street.

In 1994 a mudstone face bearing over 6,000 dinosaur tracks up to 80 cm (32 in) in diameter, made by over 150 different species of these fascinating creatures, was discovered at Sucre's cement quarry just outside the city. Sadly, dino-crazy visitors are not actually allowed to get up close and personal with these amazing relics although it is possible to gaze through binoculars at monster footprints, before wandering among realistic life-sized models of diplodocuses, ankylosauruses and many others in the Parque Cretácico.

Cal Orck'o Dinosaur Tracks

WHEN TO GO:
November to February are the least cold months, or winter for snow sports (but warm clothing is essential at any time of year).

TOP FAMILY ATTRACTIONS:
The unmissable Tren del Fin del Mundo (End of the World train) to Tierra del Fuego National Park with its hiking trails and spectacular scenery; a visit to Mastil de General Belgrano, a remote area west of the city on Isla Redonda where it's possible to send postcards home that are officially from the end of the world; a day cruise on a sailboat in the Beagle Channel to observe wildlife (including killer whales) and wild mountain scenery; a visit to a traditional estancia (ranch); a flight over Antarctica (expensive but never to be forgotten); the Cerro Castor resort for snow sports, plus Snowcat or dog-sled rides (winter only).

YOU SHOULD KNOW:
Regular minibuses leave for the National Park, Glaciar Martial, trailhead of Laguna Esmeralda and other popular tourist destinations from a parking lot at the corner of Maipu and Fadul. The Beagle Channel was named for the ship which carried Charles Darwin on his historic voyage of discovery in the 1830s, although it was surveyed and named during HMS *Beagle*'s earlier voyage to South America.

Ushuaia

The world's most southerly city, Argentina's Ushuaia is backed by the Martial Mountains and overlooks the Beagle Channel. Its remote setting made this the location for a missionary station, penal colony and naval base. But it has now become a popular stop for cruise liners on their way to Antarctica and a holiday destination unlike any other, used as a base for hiking and winter sports. It makes even the long journey required to get (almost) to the bottom of the globe worthwhile.

The old jail has now become a museum, the Museo Maritimo y ex Presidio de Ushuaia, which includes displays on the history of the colony. Another old building giving an idea of the early days of settlement is Beban House, containing a reconstruction of the old

The End of the World Train

town. The local railway was among the infrastructure built by convicts, and makes a stirring way to see the area. A steam locomotive takes the carriages (thankfully heated) along the bank of the Río Pipo from the aptly named End of the World Station to the Tierra del Fuego National Park Station.

The national park is one of the area's major draws and includes the Martial Glacier and lakes Escondido and Fagnano. Wildlife in the area includes penguins, beavers and orcas and activities include horse riding, trekking and mountain-biking. This remote place is a testament to the determination of humans to survive in whatever conditions the planet can throw at them, although it is by no means as bleak here as you might think. Sheltered from the worst of the weather by the bay's islands, it is nevertheless a windy city. The beauty and interest of this outpost at the foot of South America certainly make for a memorable family holiday.

FOLLOWING PAGES: The town of Ushuaia

Santiago

WHEN TO GO:
The climate is mild all year round and summer lasts from November to May.
TOP FAMILY ATTRACTIONS:
A free walking tour of major city sights (but tip the guide); the Chilean Museum of Pre-Columbian Art, with informative descriptions in both English and Spanish; Parque Forestal beside the Mapocho River, home of the National Museum of Fine Arts and Modern Art Museum; Museo Artequin with its amazing glass dome and interactive exhibits; Museo Interactivo Mirador, an exciting science and technology centre for youngsters.
YOU SHOULD KNOW:
Pollution in Santiago can be unpleasant, especially at times of high humidity when smog gets trapped between the Andes and the Pacific. Adventurous families using Santiago as a base could ski in the Andes in the morning and be on a Pacific beach in the afternoon. Taking photographs inside several heritage buildings, such as Palacio Cousino or Iglesia de San Francisco, is not allowed.

In 1541 Pedro de Valdiva founded Santiago on a rocky island called Huelen Hill. Here, the Mapocho River divides before rejoining further downstream to flow across a wide plain at the foot of the mighty Andes, which form a stunning backdrop to the city. Modern Santiago has much to offer visitors. Chile's capital is a place in which there is a lot to do and see, from quiet cobbled plazas in which the family can linger over coffee and snacks to busy shopping arcades. It is also a city of contrasts where old colonial architecture stands proudly among stunning skyscrapers.

There is probably no better place to start your exploration than the Centro Historico, action-packed heart of the city (but do beware of pickpockets). In the cultural centre on the south bank of the Rio Mapocha there are art shows, concerts and cafés, while in the arty Lastarria district there are good museums, theatres and bookshops plus the romantic Cerro Santa Lucia, a former Spanish fortification which is now a hilly and labyrinthine public garden. Your next stop might be the Iglesia de San Francisco (the city's oldest church) with its macabre religious art and Baroque paintings. For something completely different try the Barrio Brasil, with its cutting edge underground arts events, galleries and music venues. Barrio Bellavista between the Mapocho River and San Cristóbal Hill is famous for bohemian life.

If it's shopping that attracts the family, the eastern areas of the city – Santiago Oriente, Victacura, Providencia and Las Condes – offer designer shopping, fine gastronomy and busy street life on wide boulevards. Or for more traditional purchases there is the Mercado Central, Santiago's legendary wholesale market, or numerous craft fairs that kids will love to explore.

Santiago is a city of contrasts where old colonial architecture stands proudly among stunning skyscrapers.

CITIES

COUNTRIES